Young Children and Language

V. J. Cook

Edward Arnold

© V. J. Cook 1979

First published 1979 by
Edward Arnold (Publishers) Ltd
41 Bedford Square, London WC1B 3DQ

British Library Cataloguing in Publication Data

Cook, Vivian James
    Young children and language.
    1. Children − Language
    I. Title
    401'.9   LB1139.L3

    ISBN 0−7131−6247−3
    ISBN 0−7131−6248−1 Pbk

This book is published in two editions. The paperback edition is sold subject to the condition that it shall not, by way of trade or otherwise, be lent, re-sold, hired out, or otherwise circulated without the publisher's prior consent in any form of binding or cover other than that in which it is published and without a similar condition including this condition being imposed upon any subsequent purchaser.

Typeset by Computacomp (UK) Ltd
Fort William, Scotland
Printed and bound in Great Britain at
The Camelot Press Ltd, Southampton

Young Children and Language

Contents

Introduction

This book presents some current ideas about children's language that are relevant to people who are involved with children under five, whether in playgroups, or nurseries, or as parents. While these ideas are based on the research that has been carried out in this field in the past two decades, the book does not presuppose any particular academic background in the reader. There are, however, booklists and references at the end for those who wish to go into children's language more deeply. The examples of children's language that are used come from my own children and from playgroups I have visited, to all of which I give my thanks. I would also like to thank those working with under-fives who have discussed the ideas in this book with me, particularly my wife Pam Cook.

1

Starting to use language

Very often we take language for granted. We do not stop to think
how much it is involved in our lives and how big the gap would
be if it were removed. This chapter looks at some of the roles that
language plays in our activities and sees how these are reflected in
the child's first attempts to speak. For instance suppose that you
are walking down a street and you overhear a conversation such
as this:

'Good morning, Mrs Jones. How are you keeping?'
'Good morning, Mrs Brown. Not too bad, I suppose.'
'Terrible weather again.'
'Yes, it is, isn't it? Well I must get to the shops before they close.'
'Goodbye, Mrs Jones.'
'Goodbye.'

Superficially nothing very much happens in this conversation.
Two people meet, they exchange greetings, they talk about the
weather, one makes an excuse for leaving, they say goodbye.
Many of the conversations we have in a day are like this. It might
seem that there was no point to them; we would all save a
tremendous amount of time if we cut them out altogether. Yet
these conversations in fact show one of the most vital uses that we
have for language – language is for meeting people, for forming
social relationships, for interacting with others. Without language
the social life of the individual and of the community would cease
to exist. Language is, then, involved at the beginning of many of
the relationships we have with people; it keeps them going; and it
may even finish them off. A particular relationship can be started
by saying 'Will you marry me?', made permanent by someone
else saying 'I pronounce you man and wife', kept going by saying
'Of course I love you, darling', and broken off with a petition for

divorce. Language makes relationships, whether informal ones through conversations and letters, or official ones through ceremonies and contracts. The conversation between the two women in the street is language used for keeping up a social relationship – being on good terms with the neighbours. Think how offended Mrs Brown would have been if she had said 'Good morning' and Mrs Jones had said nothing at all. The actual things that are said do not matter; what *is* important is the motive in saying anything at all. This may be true not only of conversations between neighbours but of summit conferences on the world economic situation; what is decided is not nearly as important as the fact that world leaders have sat round a table talking to each other. So in a typical day we use language constantly for making social relationships and for maintaining them. We talk to our wives or husbands, our children, our bosses, our secretaries, the doctor who examines us, the man who drives the no. 14 bus. Though there are other reasons for these conversations, in all of them we are relating to other people, we are having social interaction.

Almost from birth the baby starts to learn how to have relationships with people. He soon realizes that if he smiles at his mother, she smiles back; if he makes a noise, she makes one too. He learns that his actions have an effect on other people, that something he does causes them to do something. Gradually he builds up particular chains of actions between him and the adult, particular 'routines' that he goes through, rather like the two women talking to each other in the street. In some of these routines the mother and baby do things at the same time. He learns to look at the same thing that she is looking at or to make noises while she is talking to him. In other routines the baby and mother take turns. The baby smiles, so his mother smiles, so the baby smiles back, and so on. Or the baby makes a gurgling noise, so his mother says something to him, so he gurgles again, until one of them gets bored. The mother and baby are learning to interact with each other, to form a relationship by developing particular routines. Indeed the baby soon starts to use these routines for interacting with total strangers. Hence the common sight of a baby parked in a pram outside a shop happily throwing out his toys so that the passersby can give them back to him. He has discovered that if you throw something out it gets given back; it is a routine for getting to know people.

At first language does not have anything to do with these routines so far as the baby is concerned. He does not use particular sounds to go with the routines in any systematic way. But it is not long before he learns that there are sounds that are important to particular routines. For instance most babies go through a period when they adore games of peekaboo. It is not just that it is exciting to have an adult pop round a door but it is the fact that he says 'peekaboo' as well. The baby learns to anticipate the adult's appearance by the adult's sounds; they are an important part of the game. Soon the baby himself starts to use sounds as part of these routines. The sounds that he produces are very different from the language an adult would use; a grunt may show he wants something, a whine that he does not like it. Nevertheless parents soon learn to recognize what particular sounds mean, what needs they express. Indeed eventually they may realize how the baby came to associate certain sounds with certain routines. My daughter Nicola, for instance, used to make a sort of 'eeyore' noise whenever she handed something to someone. It was some time before we realized that she was trying to say 'Here you are'. She had learnt that 'Here you are' is part of the routine for handing people things, even if her parents were hardly aware that this was so.

So, even when he can hardly say a word, the baby is building up routines for interacting with people. Like the two women in the street he has particular ways of saying 'hello' and 'goodbye'. To the baby the sounds are simply one aspect of what is going on. 'Byebye' is just as much waving the hand as it is making sounds. Gestures, words and actions go together in the social routines that he is building up. Greetings are only one way of interacting with people. The baby also discovers that he can attract attention to himself by making particular sounds. An indignant cry of 'me me me' soon gets him included in what is happening. Indeed my son Robert used the word 'Mummy' to get the attention of any adult that was around rather than his mother in particular. Having got someone's attention, you need to be able to give them a reason. So the baby learns to get what he wants through words. 'Bubbles' gets him a bath, 'chips' gets him food, 'more' gets more of the things or actions he likes. Even 'byebye' can be not so much a farewell as a hint that he wants to be left alone to get on with something. Though the baby is producing only one word at a time, he is already using language in several routines for interacting with people – greeting them, getting their attention, getting what he wants. His routines serve his social needs even at the one-word stage of language development.

But there are other reasons for using language. Suppose that you walk a bit further down the street and discover you are lost. You stop a passerby and the conversation goes something like this:

'Excuse me, could you tell me the way to the Angel?'
'Let me see. Yes, go down to the end of the road, turn right at the traffic lights and then bear left at the roundabout. Keep straight on and you'll be there in about half a mile.'
'Thank you very much.'

The people in this conversation do have to form a temporary relationship. Indeed 'Excuse me' and 'Thank you' are used precisely to smooth this relationship: a person who goes up to a stranger in the street and does not start with a polite opening phrase such as 'Excuse me' would be thought rather odd. However, the two people have never met before and are not likely to meet again. The point of their conversation is not the relationship but the exchange of information about where the Angel is. In other words language is being used here for communication, for asking and giving a piece of information. Every day people are continually communicating things to each other. We get up in the morning and the paper tells us the sports results; the children complain there are no cornflakes left; down the road we see a 'For Sale' sign on a house; we tell the clerk in the station where we are going and he tells us the price of a ticket; there's a chalked up notice in the booking hall that the trains are late because of a staff shortage. In all of these situations information has been exchanged; communication has taken place. So, as well as being used for social relationships, language is also used for communication. Indeed this use of language bulks so large in many adults' minds that they make the mistake of thinking that it is the only way of using language, a trap the child does not fall into.

Even before the baby starts using words, he uses gestures and sounds to tell us things; he points at a plane and grunts; he reaches for things. In a way he is already trying to communicate something. By the time he is using words this becomes more obvious. What kinds of thing is he trying to communicate with his first words? One way of answering this question is to look at the actual words he uses. Most of the early words are in fact the names of the people who surround him. He soon learns to call the right people 'Mummy' and 'Daddy' because they are important in his life. Food is also important and he learns to say 'milk' and 'nana' and 'bisk'. The other early words he learns mostly refer to animals — 'moo', or clothes — 'shoe-shoe', toys — 'dolly', or different kinds of transport — 'car'. But he is also interested in actions and says words like 'up' or 'fall down' about actions that happen around him. The words he uses tell us what he finds interesting and, hardly surprisingly, the things he finds interesting are the people and actions that make up his own world.

But knowing what he is interested in still does not tell us what he is trying to communicate. Unless in fact all he is doing when he looks at a duck and says 'quack-quack' is 'naming'. Most parents probably think that the child's main preoccupation is naming and that the most useful help they can provide with language at this stage is to name objects to the child. But is this all the child is doing — looking at things and saying their names? Can it be that the only thing he wants to communicate is what things are called? Many people believe that there is rather more to this one-word stage than naming. On the one hand, some of the words that the child says are also very useful to the development of relationships through language; saying 'plane' as one flies overhead is a way of getting the adult's attention. Naming may be a routine between the baby and its parents, rather like peekaboo or waving goodbye, important because it involves the adult interacting with the child rather than because it consists of naming things. On the other hand giving names to objects and actions seems a rather philosophical activity for a small baby. Can it really be so fascinating just to say the names of things? It seems more likely that the child wants to tell us something about what he sees going on around him. For example, if he is sitting in a playpen surrounded by toys why does he say 'wow-wow' rather than something else? Presumably because there is something interesting about the dog that he wants to tell us − 'I can hear a dog', for instance, or 'I like the dog best'. Rather than being a museum curator pinning labels on his collection, he is telling us his reactions to what he sees.

So the child's first words show him trying to express a few limited things about what he sees. There are two things that he chooses to comment on particularly − actions and people or objects. Some actions strike his attention; he says 'go' when he lets something drop, or 'gone' when his mother has left the room.

People who are doing things also interest him; he sees a snail coming down the path and says 'snail' or a cow and says 'moo'. But as well as noticing actions and the people who carry them out he also talks about the people and objects that are affected by the actions; he says 'bob bob' when he is given his bottle or 'shoe' when someone puts on his shoes. He may talk about people who are involved only as 'receivers'; he says 'mummy' as he gives his mother something. In one way these could be called 'naming' because the child says a word that refers to something he can see; in another way they seem to express comments about the passing scene.

Of course it is difficult to pin down what the child really means and it is easy to read things into the child's words that he does not intend to say. Nevertheless by looking at the relationships between the child's words and what is going on around him and by looking at the ways in which his language develops later, many people feel justified in saying that the child's single words are more than naming. After all suppose someone were reduced to saying one word at a time, wouldn't their language sound rather like naming? At a football match a man says 'goal' and because he is an adult people would assume that he meant something like 'That was a good goal' rather than 'That object over there is called a goal'. The reason why the child's attempts to say something seem to be naming is that he can say only one word at a time and so cannot put complicated ideas into words; he may be trying to say 'That bird is pretty' but all that comes out is 'bird'. Adults are able to organize speech in complicated way to express their ideas. A single word sounds like naming regardless of what the person is really trying to say.

So in the one-word stage the child is already starting to use language in at least two of the ways that adults do; he is using language to make relationships and to communicate even if he has different relationships and things to say from us.

There are other ways in which language is important to us. Suppose that you are still lost and looking for the Angel. As you walk along you try to remember what the helpful passer-by said to you and you mutter to yourself something like this:

'First I go to the end of the road, then I turn right. Then I – what did he say – left at the traffic lights? and then left at a roundabout and keep on going.'

The reason for this muttering is neither to form relationships nor to communicate; it is hard either to have a social relationship with yourself or to tell yourself something that you do not know. Rather it is to help you remember what the person said, in other words to think. Language is then also used for thinking. Perhaps this is the aspect of language that adults take most for granted. Our language and our thinking are so intertwined that we can seldom tell them apart or realize the ways in which they are connected. Language is used for remembering things; if we want to remember a phone number we mutter it over and over to ourselves. Language is used for making plans; we make shopping lists and agendas. Language is used for working out problems; detectives in novels always make long lists of the suspects. For adults language is bound up with thinking.

For a child too there are many connections between language and thinking. A one-word sentence like 'cake', for instance, shows that the child has mastered one crucial idea about language, that a particular combination of sounds connects with a particular object; the word 'cake' refers to a certain kind of food. When the child says 'sock' he shows that he has some idea that the sounds that make up 'sock' go together with a certain piece of clothing, when he says 'Teddy' he shows he is connecting the sounds with a particular toy. This is not to say that the child uses the words to refer to exactly the same objects as adults. Indeed children

notoriously go through a phase in which all men are 'Daddy' and
all animals are 'bow-wow'. Nevertheless the child knows the
general principle that sounds go together with things. Not only
this but he also shows he can group things together; the car he
gets into, the car he passes in the street, the car he sees in a book
are all called 'car'. To do this he has to find something that all
these objects have in common, what makes them a 'car' rather
than a 'moo' or a 'mummy'. So a second principle he has
acquired is that things can be put into groups. Even these two
principles depend on a more basic aspect of his thinking. Piaget
has suggested that one of the crucial things that a baby has to
learn is what objects are like. One important thing is that they
continue to exist when we cannot see them. However, a young
baby loses interest if something is hidden from him and will not
bother to look for it. This may mean that because he cannot see it
he thinks it does not exist any more. So if a child asks for 'cake'
this shows that he is aware that more cake exists. Language for
social relationships grows out of routines the child uses before he
can talk. But his first words also depend on some of the ways that
he has learnt to think. Language is not separate but depends upon
many aspects of the child's development.

However, there is a difference between saying that the child's
words depend upon his thinking and saying that the child is using
language for thinking, like the person muttering the directions to
the Angel. For it is not just that the thinking of adults depends on
language; rather it is that they use language itself to help them
think. While the child's language is dependent on his thinking, at
an early age he does not use language itself as a tool. For instance
adults are used to controlling their actions through language; a
pilot goes through a checking routine before take-off; a sportsman
goes over a list of do's and don't's in his head. But language does
not control the actions of young children; saying something does
not necessarily help them to do it, even if they are perfectly aware
of what they are saying. The relationships between language and
thinking are complicated and will be dealt with more fully in
chapter 4. For the moment the point about language and thinking
at the one-word stage is that, while the language the child uses
depends upon his ways of thinking, he does not yet use language
to help his thinking.

There is one more way of using language that is important to the child. One of the songs that my children liked to sing went:

Brown girl in the ring tra la la la la
There's a brown girl in the ring, tra la la la la la
Brown girl in the ring, tra la la la la
She looks like a sugar in a plum, plum, plum.

Whatever the words of the song may mean to the writer or singer they do not communicate anything much to my children. Instead the words of the song have an emotional affect because of the sounds and rhythm. When language is used in this way it doesn't matter so much what is said as how it is said; the sounds and rhythms are more important than the meaning. This is language used for play, language for its own sake with nothing to communicate. Adults play with language all the way from the heights of poetry to the depths of the pun. Language can be used as an end in itself.

To the small child also language can be play. It is not just that he uses language while he is playing, for the purpose of this may be to interact with people, to tell them things or to put his thoughts into words. Instead the use of language for play means the child playing with language itself just as he plays with a toy or anything else that takes his fancy. A good example of this comes long before the baby starts to use words when he goes through the 'babbling' stage. This is when babies produce long strings of sounds for no other apparent reason than that they enjoy doing it. So far is it from being language that they do it more when they are by themselves than when they are with others. But though the purpose seems play babbling is nevertheless connected with language development. It used to be believed that babbling sounds were made more or less at random; the child was trying out all the sounds he could make with his mouth and tongue. However, by listening carefully to babbling, people have found that there is a connection between the sounds the baby uses for babbling and those he uses in speech much later. For instance babies tend to start their babbling noises with a consonant sound like 'k' or 'b' much more often than they finish them with a consonant. This is exactly what is found in the child's first words, where he tends to use consonants at the beginning of words but to leave them out at the end so that he says 'bir' rather than 'bird' or 'pea' rather than 'peach'. The baby's attempts at playing with language-sounds in babbling lead to the sounds that he uses in his early speech. In the one-word stage too he delights in saying and listening to nonsense words of different kinds. My son for instance used to say 'liddle liddle liddle' when he was riding on people's knees and join in choruses of 'Old Macdonald' with 'ee ah, ee ah'.

The thread running through this chapter has been that from the beginning the child has different uses for language – making relationships, telling people things, expressing his thoughts, and playing. Of course there are other ways of describing the child's uses of language than these four; different people have drawn up different lists of the child's uses of language and how they develop. Nevertheless, whichever way one looks at it, it is still true that young children have several things that they want to do through language. Language development is therefore hard to separate from other aspects of the child's development. Physical development for instance – the child needs to be able to control his breathing, his mouth, his tongue, and other muscles quite precisely before he can produce the sounds of speech. Mental development – ways of thinking are reflected in speech and later on language is used for thinking. Social development as well – language reflects and influences his relationships with the people around him. While in later chapters, various aspects of language are discussed separately, it must not be forgotten that they are all connected. Even in this chapter it may have seemed as if the ways in which we use language are completely separate, that language is used sometimes for one reason, sometimes for another. But the true picture is that in adults it may be used for several reasons at the same time. Mrs Jones's remark, 'terrible weather again', is just a polite phrase to pass the time of day, but even so it communicates a small piece of information about the weather, however trivial it may be.

The fact that language development has many sides also means that it is hard to say exactly when the child starts to use language. His routines with his mother start with noises and movements and gradually come to include language but it is impossible to pinpoint a single moment as the beginning of language. The same with babbling; the baby is using sounds in some of the ways he will use later in speech, so has he then started language? Even looking at whether the baby can hear certain speech sounds does not provide a clear moment when language begins. For instance, experiments have shown that babies a month old can tell the difference between the sounds 'pa' and the sounds 'ba' but it seems absurd to say that they have started language. Parents have usually dated the beginning of language from the 'first word' they can recognize in the baby's speech. Unfortunately spotting the first word depends on the parent's skill or imagination at working out the child's speech and in any case there is no real reason why the ability to say one word should be the crucial start of language rather than some other aspect. Different sides of language develop out of different aspects of the child's life and so there may be different moments when the child starts each aspect of language.

For the same reason it can be dangerous to pin different stages of language down to different ages. Children go through the same stages in the same order but the age at which they start and the pace at which they progress can vary very much. So in this book though ages are mentioned from time to time there is no attempt to give a precise series of dates that the 'normal' child follows. For this means giving an average date when children reach a particular stage. By definition an average means that half the children have reached it by this particular date and half of them reach it later. Half the parents who read these dates for 'normal' children worry because their children are backward, half are pleased because they are advanced for their age. But the age at which particular children reach particular stages of language varies immensely; the fact that one child is later than others at reaching a particular language milestone does not necessarily have anything to do with backwardness. Einstein for instance is said not to have spoken until the age of three.

2

Starting to organize sentences

Suppose that you turn on the radio and you hear the announcer say 'Arsenal beat West Ham one nil after extra time'; you have no problem in understanding what he means and you know the result of the football match. Suppose, however, you had turned on your radio and heard instead 'Time West beat Ham extra one after Arsenal nil'; this time you might guess that the announcer was talking about football but you wouldn't really know what he was trying to say, let alone the result of the match. The difference between these two announcements is that the first one uses the normal English order of words; the second is English words in a jumbled order. One makes sense to a speaker of English because he knows the ways in which English sentences are organized; the other is nonsense because it is not organized in any familiar way. Adults seldom pay much attention consciously to the organization of what they are saying; all they are aware of is trying to convey their meaning in the ways that seem natural to them. They forget that they have had to learn these 'natural' ways and that their 'natural' ways of organizing sentences seem strange and unnatural to people who speak another language. To make sense the words in a sentence have to be put together in particular ways − to be organized.

One particular way in which English sentences are organized is the order of the words. The fact that one word comes in front of another conveys an important part of what the speaker wants to say. Take the first announcement, 'Arsenal beat West Ham one nil after extra time.' A person who speaks English knows that Arsenal were the winners because the word 'Arsenal' comes before the word 'beat'; he knows that West Ham lost because 'West Ham' comes after 'beat'. If the order of words were changed, he would understand something different. 'West Ham beat Arsenal' means that West Ham won and Arsenal lost. In English a change in the order of words can change the meaning of a sentence; 'Elizabeth loves Richard' does not mean the same as 'Richard loves Elizabeth' even though the words are the same. The most important thing that is usually shown by the word order of the sentence is who is doing something, and who or what it is done to – who is loving and who is loved. But word order can also show other things. For instance we know that Arsenal scored one goal and West Ham none, because the score that is given first belongs to the first team mentioned and the second score to the second team. Again a change of word order means a change of meaning. But sometimes the English language will allow only one order of words; a change in word order produces a peculiar sentence rather than changing the meaning. In 'After extra time' for instance the word 'after' has to come before the word 'extra' and the word 'time' has to come last. Any other combinations such as 'after time extra' or 'time after extra' are meaningless.

So the child has to learn that sentences are organized and are not just random combinations of words. Eventually he has to know the whole system of organizing sentences that the adult uses without thinking. To start with, the child tries organizing sentences in simple ways to express his needs and ideas. At the one-word stage the child doesn't have much opportunity for organising sentences. The most he can do towards the end of this stage is to connect his single words together into some kind of sequence. My son for example said 'Me. Me. Bob. Bob. More' when he wanted more milk in his bottle. He had made a sequence of 'me', which he used to catch people's attention, 'bob', his word for bottle, and 'more'. But the words are still not combined together; they come out as separate items.

As soon as the child can say two words, he has a greater opportunity for conveying his meaning by combining his two words together. Developing from one word to two words does not, though, mean that he changes the ways in which he uses language; rather he uses language for the same purposes as before. But the fact that he can say two words means that he can convey more complicated messages and make their meaning more obvious. In the first months of life the baby and the mother learn to look at things together; later his single words like 'me' serve to attract attention to things he is looking at. Now that he can say two words he can get the adult to pay attention to whatever interests him more effectively by saying 'see water' or 'look lolly'. He has a kind of two-word formula for attracting our attention; start with 'look' or 'see' and then say the word referring to the object you're interested in, such as 'water' or 'lolly'. Using this formula he finds that grown-ups react in a satisfying way to his cries of 'look car', 'look womble', 'look beads', 'look daddy', and the other combinations he thinks up. So one of the routines between the child and adult is to draw each other's attention to interesting things that they see; the adult finds it natural to say 'look at that pretty doggie over there', the child to say 'look plane'. In a way this is 'naming' except that it is more like drawing attention to things than giving them names. It is a routine for interacting with people that develops out of earlier routines; language simply makes it more effective.

The other things he does with language are similarly expanded at the two-word stage. Getting people's attention is one way of getting them to do things and the child can get things done more effectively with a two-word formula in which he combines a word for an action with a word for an object. So he says 'be pig' or 'draw Womble'. In particular he has a two-word formula for getting something that consists of the word 'more' followed by a word referring to whatever it is he is after — 'more Babar', 'more marmite', or 'more nut'. These sentences with 'more' are not so much describing what he sees as requesting something he wants; 'more bubbles' is a request for a bath not a comment on a pile of bubbles. Even the child's use of language for greeting people benefits by his ability to say two words; he now says 'hello daddy' or 'bye-bye Chigley'.

So far as using language to meet people is concerned, it is not necessary to organize the sentence in very complicated ways. It's another matter when one turns to the use of language for communication. There the sentence may have to be organized in complex ways to get the idea across. Again there is no clear break between the child using language for communication at the one-word stage and at the two-word. At the one-word stage he commented on actions and the people or objects involved in them but could only talk about them one at a time. The advantage of being able to use two words is that he can express slightly more and can combine two words together. He doesn't have many new things to say but he can tell us more about them. So instead of mentioning either the person who does the action or the action but not both, he has a formula in which he mentions the person and the action. 'Slug coming' he says as he plays out Dr Who; 'Lance dead' when the person he's playing with pretends to be dead; 'daddy sleep' when his father is sleeping. Another formula combines the action and the person or object affected by it. He says 'hurt mouth' when someone has hurt his mouth or 'pull hair' when they have pulled his hair. But, as well as talking about what people or things do and have done to them, he now starts to talk about where they are and where they are going. The formula for this consists of a word for a person or object combined with a word like 'here' that refers to a place or a direction. 'Here book' tells us where the book is, 'carry loo' is a request to be carried to the toilet. This formula includes a new ingredient – talking about where things are.

Though at the two-word stage he still wants mostly to talk about the people and objects around him, he can do so in different ways. He can for instance develop his 'naming' routine by pointing to things and saying 'that car'. He describes things by saying 'pretty car' or 'funny dalek'. He tells us who things belong to by saying 'mine biscuit' or 'mummy nose'. The formula for these is to combine a word for a person or object with a word describing it. But the same formula can also express the idea that something does not exist. This is managed by combining the word 'no' with another word, to get 'no baby'. Usually this formula is a way of commenting that something he would normally expect to see is not in its usual place. So 'no baby' is said when he peers into a pram to find it empty, 'no pictures' when he picks up an adult book. The adult uses 'no' in many other ways but for the child the idea of unexpected absence is uppermost in his mind. A similar formula expresses the idea that something has gone or disappeared; 'allgone milk' comments on his milk being finished. A formula using the word 'more' expresses the same idea of absence except that it is a demand to the adult to do something about it; 'more marmite' is a request for more rather than a statement of fact. So at the two-word stage people feel that the child is not combining words at random but has a certain limited number of formulas that he uses. The ones mentioned here are typical of children at this stage but of course any individual child may have slightly different formulas of his own. But does this mean that the child appreciates the importance of word order or that he is just putting the words in any order? In fact the child does seem to be aware of word order. He says 'see Womble' not 'Womble see' when he tries to attract our attention, 'more milk' rather than 'milk more' when he tries to get something he wants. Though this may not be deliberate, the child uses the same order whenever he uses the same formula. My own children, for instance, always attracted one's attention with 'see car', never with 'car see'. In many cases this order is the same as an adult would use; 'Help jelly' looks different from the adult sentence 'Can you help me to some jelly?' but in both of them 'help' comes before 'jelly'. Indeed almost all the examples of children's sentences in this chapter have had the same order as adult sentences. 'Slug coming' has the same order as 'The slugs are coming', 'No pictures' as 'There aren't any pictures'. It is the extra words in the adult sentences that hide this similarity.

Too much must not be made of this point as there is the ever-present danger of reading too much in to the child's speech. Sometimes the child's sentence is so different from the adult's that is is impossible to say whether it has the same order. What adult sentence should one compare with 'allgone milk'? Often the similarity between the child's and the adult's sentences depends on which adult sentence is chosen. 'Go train' looks like the adult order of words if it is compared to 'I want to go in the train' but looks quite different if it is compared to 'The train is going'. Nevertheless on the occasions when one can be reasonably certain what the child means to say by looking at what is going on and knowing what interests him, he seems to have definite ways of putting two-word sentences together and the order of words that he uses is similar to the word order of adults.

Important as the order of words is to English, it is only one of the ways in which the sentence is organized. In other languages, such as German, it is less important than in English. One of the other ways of organizing the sentence is through link words and word endings. To go back to the child's sentence 'slug coming', this is different from 'The slugs are coming' because it does not have the link-words 'the' and 'are' and the word ending '-s'. 'Carry loo' is different from 'carry me to the loo' because it does not have 'me', 'too', and 'the'; 'mummy nose' is different from 'That is Mummy's nose' because it does not have 'that', 'is' and the word ending '-s'. In the adult sentences the words are joined together with these link words and word endings. Link words such as 'the' and 'at' or word endings like '-s' and '-ing' allow the adult to show how words are connected. But at the two-word stage these are hardly ever used by the child. His sentences have the bones but not the flesh. The only way they can be organized is through word order.

As the child's sentences get longer, he starts to put flesh on the bones, to use link words and word endings. Usually he learns these in a particular sequence. The one he learns first is the ending '-ing' as in 'mummy crying' or 'Julie working'. Next come the link words 'in' and 'on' as in 'light on' and 'on telly'. Then comes the plural '-s' in sentences such as 'nice eyes' or 'daleks in there'. Then irregular forms of verbs such as 'came', the possessive '-s', and some forms of 'to be'. Next the word 'the' as in 'the tree'. Then come 'am', 'are' and so on combined with '-ing' to make sentences such as 'I'm climbing up' and 'You're splashing.' Step by step the child adds more of these words and word endings to his speech. There is no need to go through the long list of them provided the point has been made that they are learnt in a sequence that does not vary much from one child to another. Though there are differences in how fast children go through the sequence, the sequence itself remains more or less the same. For some time the child continues to use more and more of these in his sentences.

This chapter has looked at some early stages in the child's development from the point of view of making relationships and communicating. What about the other uses of language? So far as language for thinking is concerned, the child's two-word sentences show some of the ways in which he is thinking. Combining a person and an action in 'Daddy sleep' or putting 'no' with an object as in 'no baby' gives certain clues about the way his mind works, the concepts he has acquired. But he is still not using language as a way of helping him to think.

He also continues to play with language. One mother used to record what her son said as he was falling asleep and she would find long monologues such as: 'Stop. Have to stop. Stop. Stop it. Stop the ball please. Take it. Stop it. You take it. Please take it.' Here the child seems to be playing with combining words together in different ways. He takes a particular formula and he tries it out for its own sake just as he tries out different ways of arranging bricks.

So by this stage of development the child is starting to organize sentences. Obviously he still has a long way to go. But the foundations are already there. He is using word order; he is beginning to use link words and word endings; he uses language in several different ways. Already he has taken the important first steps towards adult language. Small as these steps may seem, they are still a considerable achievement for the child, one that no machine yet invented can duplicate, and few, if any, animals.

3

Developing up to five

The last two chapters described two important principles about language that the child learns quite soon. One is that language is used for many reasons, the other that it is organized in various ways. After he has learnt these principles his development up to the age of five largely consists of learning more of the reasons for using language and more of the ways in which language is organized. This is far more demanding than it sounds because of the complexity of a language such as English. For instance English speakers say 'bigger' and 'more beautiful', rather than 'more big' or 'beautifuller'. The reason is that '-er' is added to short words, 'more' goes before longer words. This is something that they have learnt about English. They also say 'Have you got *any* stamps?' but 'Yes I've got *some*' and 'No I haven't got *any*'. The rule of thumb to explain this is that 'any' is used in questions and with negatives, 'some' in other sentences. Again something that the adult has learnt which he probably doesn't even know he has learnt. These are just two examples of the kinds of thing the child has to learn; English has many, many of them. In time the child learns them all, even if there are long periods in which he says 'more better' or 'I haven't got some'. Though the child is not perhaps making major discoveries about language during this time, the sheer quantity and complexity of what he is learning should not be underestimated. For this reason, while the first two chapters gave fairly complete accounts of the earliest stages, this chapter, which looks at the child's development up to five, chooses some of the more important aspects of this rather than trying to talk about all of them.

The first half of this chapter takes up the theme of word order. To recap what was said earlier, at the two-word stage more often than not the child uses the same order of words as the adult. The child hitting his mother for calling him a baby and insisting 'no baby' is using the same order as 'I'm not a baby', whatever other differences there are. One of the important aspects of word order in English is that usually the person who is doing something is mentioned first, then comes a verb, and the person or object that is affected by the action is mentioned after the verb. So 'Margaret dislikes Edward' suggests that Margaret is the person who is disliking someone and Edward is the person who is disliked. The child's sentence 'You bang nose' has the same order and suggests the same relationship between 'you', the person who is banging, and 'nose', the object that was banged. At the two-word stage the child may be able to express only two of these three things but he nevertheless puts them in the same order as the adult, as in 'water run', when water is running into a basin, and 'making rounds', when a boy is running round and round.

However, there is more to the order of the sentence in English than this. In particular there are two ways in which people or objects can be affected by actions and the difference between these is shown by word order. In the sentence 'Penny gave John a book' the order shows that John received the book and that it was the book that changed hands. In general the person who receives something is mentioned before the object that is given – 'John' comes before 'a book'. The child has therefore to learn what the word order means when two persons or objects are mentioned after the verb. About the age of five he in fact makes a rather curious mistake; he thinks that the one that is mentioned first is the object that is affected and the one that comes second is the person who receives it. If you show the child some toys and say 'Give the man the dog', you find that he gives the man to the dog rather than the dog to the man, as would be natural for an adult. So he understands the word order in exactly the opposite fashion to the adult. Of course much of the time the child's common sense tells him what he is supposed to do; if his mother says 'Give mummy the fork' he is hardly likely to try to pick her up and stand her on the fork. But, when the only clues he has to go on are word order, he persistently makes this mistake.

The reason for this is that there is another way of saying exactly the same thing in English but with a different word order. As well as 'Penny gave John a book' we can also say 'Penny gave a book to John.' The order of 'John' and 'a book' has been reversed and the link word 'to' has been added. So, in this alternative word order, the object that is given is mentioned first and the person who receives it is mentioned second. The child of five who has such problems understanding 'Give the man the car' has no problem at all with 'Give the car to the man'. He has latched on to one of the two word orders that occur in English. He understands 'Give the man the dog' as if it were 'Give the man to the dog' and does not see the importance of the link word 'to'. The child is still learning about the word order in English sentences. He fails to see that there are two possible word orders here and that the clue to which one is being used is the word 'to'. Even up to ten children still have trouble with this when they cannot fall back on their common sense.

In this case there are two variations of word order which the child cannot tell apart. Another striking variation from the standard word order is questions. A common way of asking a question is to use a different word order. 'Are you coming out this evening?' is different from 'You are coming out this evening' because the word 'are' comes before 'you' instead of after. The usual way of asking questions is to have a verb such as 'is' or 'can' at the beginning of the sentence, as in 'Is it raining?' where 'is' comes before 'it' or 'Have you been to New York?' where 'have' comes before 'you'. So, while an ordinary sentence has the person who is doing something mentioned before the verb, in a question such as 'Are the children out in the garden?' the verb comes before the name of the person. Another important thing about questions is that many of them use 'question words' such as 'where', 'who' or 'what' which usually come first in the sentence. So there are two things the child has to learn about questions; one is the difference in word order; the other is the use of question words.

The child soon learns to put question words in the right place. My son Robert was saying 'Where Nicola?', 'What Nicola doing?' and 'Where Julie gone?' well before he was two and a half. As with link words, the child does not learn all the question words at once. He starts by using 'what' and 'where' and then goes on to 'why', 'how', and 'when'. But he learns to use the special word order for questions after he learns to use question words. Many children go through a stage when they say sentences such as 'What it is?' rather than 'What is it?' The question word is in the right place but the order is wrong.

So with questions the child has to learn an important exception to the standard word order, namely that the verb comes before the name of the person. The child hears many questions and it does not take him long to learn their word order. But there are other sentences with special word orders which the child hears less often and which elude him for much longer. For instance 'Goldilocks was found by the three bears in their bedroom.' Here, although Goldilocks is mentioned first, she is not the person who is carrying out the action; instead she is affected by it and the three bears, who are mentioned after the verb, are those responsible. The order here is the opposite to the usual one 'The three bears found Goldilocks in the bedroom'. The clues to this are the special form of the verb, 'was found' rather than 'find', and the link-word 'by'. The child probably does not hear this kind of sentence very often since it usually comes in written English when the writer is trying to convey factual information, whether in football reports in the daily papers or scientific articles. The child does not realize that this kind of sentence has a special order and so he misunderstands it. If you ask him to show what is happening when you say 'Tom was kicked by Mary', he will act out Tom kicking Mary. Of course his common sense often tells him what is right even if he does not know the word order. After all everybody knows that it was the three bears that found Goldilocks, not vice versa. But when he has no other clues he falls back on the word order that he has already learnt and arrives at the wrong answer. Only between four and five do children start to appreciate the clues that these sentences are different. By five the child has mastered most of these special word orders and knows the kinds of variations from the usual order that are allowed in English. His ways of organizing sentences have become almost as sophisticated as the adult's.

The second half of this chapter is about the ways in which the child develops language for social purposes up to five. At an early stage the child uses routines in which he alternates speaking and listening; he takes turns. But a true conversation is not just taking turns, it is trying to see what the other person is after, to understand his point of view as well as your own. At first this two-sided kind of conversation does not appeal to the child. He is using language to get attention and to satisfy his own needs rather than to understand the other person. The child does not see himself as one person among a crowd of people, but as the unique centre of the universe. Other people are not individuals with lives of their own but are important only when they affect him. One experiment shows how this affects his language. If children under four are given different combinations of the same three words such as 'boy girl push' or 'push girl boy' or 'girl boy push', one of the ways in which they react is to push both the girl and boy dolls. In other words they think of themselves as being the people to carry out the actions, not anybody named in the sentence; although the sentence has not even mentioned the child, he thinks he is the most important person in it! Most people feel that at this stage language has to be directly useful to the child and to satisfy his own needs. He finds it difficult to see the other person's point of view. Other people, however, feel that the language even in his simple routines nevertheless shows some signs that he can appreciate the give and take of conversation.

Let us see how this ability to relate to other people through language develops up to five. For a change let us look at a playgroup situation since this shows the child in contact with a wider range of people, not just his own family but children his own age and less familiar adults. One simple thing that stands out is who the child talks to, who he relates with. At $2\frac{1}{2}$ for instance he spends as much time in a playgroup or nursery talking to adults as he spends talking to children. Much of the time he is calling directly for the adult's attention – 'look at me' – or telling tales about his companions – 'Christopher won't slide.' At 5, however, he is talking to other children at least twice as much as he talks to adults. This change shows how he gradually relates to a wider range of people through language, children as well as adults.

Something similar is seen if one looks at what children say to each other in the playgroup. Many people have noticed that in the early stages when children play together they do not so much talk to each other as have separate monologues. Three children that I saw playing with sand said 'build it up to the top yeah', 'water going to go in that little hole,' and 'I'll go and fetch some shells.' Though each of these remarks sounds as if the child is talking to the others, in fact each of them describes what the child is doing or planning. Much of the language in this kind of play is a commentary on what they are doing, possibly imitating the kinds of thing that their mothers and playgroup leaders say to them. Other remarks by the same children were 'We're playing in the nice sandy', 'I'm playing in the water' and 'I'm blowing bubbles in my bottle'. Sometimes these commentaries overlap with appeals for adult attention or approval; blowing bubbles or sailing down the slide may be something to boast about. But mostly they sound as if the child is using language for his own benefit rather than talking to other people.

As the child becomes more aware of other individuals he uses language more to boost his own confidence. A child playing with playdough says 'I've got lots' and another child immediately replies 'I've got lots too'. Balancing on top of a climbing frame the child announces 'I can stand up here'. Playing with Lego, one child insists 'That's mine' while another retaliates 'You must let me have one.' Once you realize that other people exist you have to protect your own rights against them – 'I haven't got some space' – or claim that your own possessions are better than anybody else's – 'I've got a big one.' This kind of language increases sharply about the age of $3\frac{1}{2}$ and after that remains at about the same level. Learning that other people have rights makes you stand up for your own.

The growing independence from adults in the playgroup setting also means that the child plays more *with* other children rather than *alongside* them. Children start to cooperate in play with each other rather than being individuals who happen to be sharing the same piece of play equipment. The child uses language to collaborate with other children; he says 'Come on, let's stand up and do it' or 'You go on and I'll look after it.' While dressing up the children organize their roles:

'Here a police hat. We are fire-engine men.'
'I'm a pirate.'
'No, you're not.'

The child is becoming more part of a group and able to cooperate with others, and less an individual whose only concern is for himself. He plays out roles such as firemen or mothers in which he deliberately adopts the language suitable for the role – 'naughty girl, you're a naughty girl'. Up to five there is a large increase in this kind of collaborative language where children cooperate and pay attention to what others are saying. Just before five another step occurs in which the child can not only agree with other children in collaborative play but can also disagree or deny what another child is saying – 'You've got two books. You can't have two books.' Playing with others is no longer just submerging yourself in the group but asserting yourself within the group.

One other change before five is more connected with mental than social development. This is using language for giving reasons. My son, for example, announced at about five while he was pretending to be a rabbit 'You can't go down my hole because it's too small for you.' Again when his mother was turning on the gas cooker he said 'Mummy too much – I'll get burned.' Both of these remarks try to explain things, to give reasons why they happen. In a playgroup I've heard exchanges such as:

'Could I have that?'
'No.'
'Well I haven't got nothing.'

Rather than simply asserting his rights the child is giving a reason why he should be given something.

This chapter has followed the child's language up to about the age of five. Again it should be mentioned that it has taken only two threads out of the many that run through the child's development. Nevertheless these two are undoubtedly important; the child has now mastered the ways in which sentences are organized, with certain exceptions, and has learnt how to use language for social purposes in groups of other children. The next chapter sees how this is connected to the child's mental development.

4

Meaning, thinking, and language

One starting point for looking at the development of meaning in the child's language is to take a pair of opposites such as 'up' and 'down'. In one respect these words couldn't be more different, in another respect they have something in common – they both refer to the direction in which something moves. 'I went down the road' or 'Jack and Jill went up the hill' talk about the direction in which people are moving. Indeed this is the aspect of their meaning that the child learns first; he says 'more up' or 'up-down' when he wants to be bounced up and down or he uses 'up' to mean movement either up or down. Later he learns that 'up' is for upward movement, 'down' for downward movement. There is a disconcerting stage when he seems to use a word to mean its opposite, to say 'up' when he means down. But in fact the child is perfectly consistent according to his lights; 'up' is movement regardless of direction. The same is true of other pairs of words such as 'before' and 'after', and 'more' and 'less'. The child learns something that they have in common – that 'before' and 'after' are about time, 'more' and 'less' about quantity – but he has not necessarily learnt the differences between them. So he sometimes thinks that 'before' means the same as 'after' and that 'more milk' means the same as 'less milk'.

For, like 'up' and 'down', most words do not have one simple meaning; they are made up of several bits of meaning. If you ask someone to tell you what a house is, they might say 'It's a building where somebody lives.' The meaning of the word 'house' is made up of two other bits – 'building' and 'where somebody lives'. The meaning of 'house' is different from the meaning of 'church', which combines the same bit 'building' with another bit 'where people go to worship', and different also from 'caravan', which combines 'vehicle' with 'where somebody lives'. Indeed if you look up almost any word in the dictionary you find that the definition gives several bits of meaning that together make up the meaning of the word. Looking up 'car' in a recent dictionary for instance I found 'A vehicle with three or usually four wheels and driven by a motor, especially one for carrying people'. Each bit of this definition is important and contributes to the meaning of the word. If the vehicle had two wheels it would be a motorcycle; if it didn't carry people it would be a van; and if it didn't have a motor it certainly wouldn't be a car. One way of looking at the child's development of meaning is to see how he acquires these bits of meaning. So far as 'up' and 'down' are concerned he first learns the bit 'movement' and later adds the bits 'upwards' and 'downwards'. The same when he learns the word 'dog'; first of all he learns that it has four legs and so he uses it for cats and horses and anything that has four legs; then he learns other bits of its meaning such as the fact that it barks and chases cats and so on. Even with the word 'daddy' he may think this means only 'man' and use it for any male and only later learn the other important part of the meaning, namely that it's a man in a particular relationship to him. So one theory is that children pick up the meanings of words one bit at a time. They don't acquire the whole meaning of a word when they first start using it but learn the meaning bit by bit.

Often, although the child is using the adult word apparently correctly, he means something different from us. My son used to say 'I've got a headache' and we assumed that he knew what he was talking about. It was only when he said 'I've got a headache in my tummy' that we realized that 'headache' meant something different to him. Appearances can be deceptive; the fact that the child seems to use the word in the same way as an adult is no guarantee that he means the same thing. It is only when he happens to use it in a situation where his own meaning stands out that this becomes obvious. Very often of course this doesn't happen. Take the words 'big' and 'old'. I am certain that for many children these have almost the same meaning; a big person is also in their terms usually an old person; an older child is usually bigger than a younger child. But there may never be an occasion when the child says something that gives away his peculiar meaning for 'old'. After all in his experience of the world bigger people usually *are* older people and so he will seem to use the word quite properly. But to the adult the connection between size and age is almost coincidence; it isn't necessary for a 'big' man to be an 'old' man – indeed almost the opposite might be said to happen after a certain age. The child seizes on an aspect that he believes is crucial to the meaning of a word but that may be almost irrelevant to the adult. For instance, it has been suggested that the child's idea of the difference between the meaning of 'man' and 'woman' must be rather different from the adult's. The child may well use the words correctly and never say 'man' when he means 'woman' and vice versa. But to him the difference is probably a matter of the clothes they wear, the hairstyles they have, the things they say or do, and so on, with the biological differences being just a small part. The most important differences that strike the child between men and women are probably the superficial ones of appearance and behaviour. Unless we are careful the child may indeed think that the crucial meaning of 'girl' is 'child who plays with dolls and wears dresses' and be at the mercy of the various stereotypes of sex roles that people have drawn attention to in recent years.

Sometimes the bits of meaning that the child learns are the same as those that add up to the adult's meaning, sometimes they are different. Why then does the child learn one bit rather than another? Why do his bits differ from ours? What makes him single out 'having four legs' as the important bit in the meaning of the word 'dog' rather than 'makes a barking noise' or 'chases cats'? The main explanation is that some things strike his attention more than others. The bits of meaning that he learns reflect the things that he has noticed about his surroundings. For example, to go back to pairs of opposites, the child quite soon learns the link words 'in' and 'on' and produces them in his speech in ways that suggest he knows what they mean. If you try giving him a cup and a sugar-lump and say to him 'Put the sugar-lump in the cup', he understands what he has to do. But with a child of about two, if you turn the cup upside down and say again 'Put the sugar-lump in the cup', you are in for a surprise. For the child will now put it on top of the cup rather than inside; his meaning for 'in' seems to be the same as his meaning for 'on'. The reason is that he is basing his meaning of 'in' on his past experience. Usually cups are the right way up and he has never been asked to put things inside them when they are upside down. His meaning depends on what he has experienced and on the ways he is used to perceiving what is going on around him. One principle underlying the child's development of meaning is, then, the ways in which he sees his surroundings. Everybody he sees can be classified as a man or a woman by their appearance and actions and so he thinks this normal feature of his surroundings must be the magic clue to the difference between 'man' and 'woman'.

Another example of this came in the last chapter which gave the order in which question words are learnt, starting with 'what' and 'where' and going on to 'why', 'how', and 'when'. The reason for the early appearance of 'what' and 'where' is that they arise naturally out of the child's activities as he talks about his toys and where they are. Chapter 2 found that even at the two-word stage the child was starting to talk about where things were. 'Why' and 'when' are more abstract ideas that depend on the child also knowing about cause and effect and about time; hence they are learned later. As the child's attention may be drawn to all kinds of features of his surroundings, the bits of meaning that he learns are also of different types. It is not that he always starts from the most general aspect of meaning and then learns particular aspects, or that the reverse is true; sometimes he does one, sometimes the other. Nevertheless one group of people believe that the child starts with 'simple' meanings which he gradually adds together to get more complicated ones. The order in which the child learns link words and word endings can be explained by saying that the child learns the simple ones before he learns the more complicated ones that combine together the meanings of the simple ones. Thus the child learns the word ending '-s' which goes on the verb, as in 'he goes', after he learns the plural '-s' in 'books' and the past '-ed' in 'watched' because, some people claim, the meaning of the '-s' in 'goes' depends upon the ideas that are found in the other two.

The child may mean different things from the adult, partly because he possesses only part of the adult meaning, partly because he has limited experience of the world. This leads us into the links between the child's language and his thinking. How does his meaning reflect his ways of thinking?

Suppose that a young child looks at a toy car and says the word 'red'. He seems to have learnt how to use the word 'red'; he is connecting the sounds that make up 'red' with a particular colour. So the idea of a red colour and the word 'red' must be linked in his mind. But how are they linked? On the one hand it might be that the child first learns the idea of 'redness' and then acquires the word 'red' to describe it; his use of the word depends upon him already knowing the idea of 'redness'. On the other hand he might know the word 'red' and acquire the idea of 'redness' by hearing the word used in connection with a particular colour; in this case his idea of 'redness' depends upon him knowing the word 'red'.

This is the major problem when talking about how language is connected to thinking – does the way we think influence our language or does our language influence the way we think?

The reason why this is important is that these two possibilities lead to different conclusions about bringing up the child. If language comes first, then language itself must be treated as the foundation on which the child builds his thinking. At home and school our chief task is therefore to help the child's language as everything else follows from his language development. If on the other hand thinking comes first, language will play a more subordinate role and our job is to help the child to think; once he can think the language will follow. To put it in terms of colour, a teacher might decide to teach the child the word 'red' by getting him to practice understanding and saying colour-names with a set of coloured bricks; or the teacher might set the bricks out in front of him and ask him to sort them out into different colours without mentioning particular colour-names. The choice for the teacher is whether to concentrate on language or on thinking. The snag in making this choice is that there is not a single neat 'Yes' or 'No' to the question of whether language or thinking is more basic. Some aspects of language lead to some aspects of thought and some aspects of thinking to some aspects of language. These links also vary according to the age of the child; at the early stages the child's language may be based on his thinking, at later stages, for instance in the teens, the reverse may be true.

But most of all our answer to the question depends on what we mean by 'thinking'. Taken at its most general, thinking is not so much the conscious thoughts that pass through our minds as the whole system that organizes how we behave and see the world. Adults have characteristic ways of looking at things which are different from those of children, as can be seen from any exhibition of children's drawings. Perspective, for instance, is not part of the child's way of seeing the world. The differences between the child's systems of thought and the adult's are profound but it is only occasionally that this becomes obvious from the child's behaviour. Piaget carried out many experiments that demonstrate the systems of thought of the child under seven. One famous example is the tall thin glass and the short fat glass that contain exactly the same amount of water. If a young child is asked which has the most water, he says the tall one even if he sees water being poured from one to the other before his very eyes. Another experiment consists of two rows of objects evenly spaced apart; the child correctly says that they both have the same number of objects. But squash one of the lines up and the child says that the longer one now has more in it. People have disagreed over the explanation for this behaviour but whichever explanation is true these experiments show in a striking way how the child behaves in a different way from the adult. It would never occur to an adult to give the child's answers and he cannot see how they make sense. As well as thinking in different ways from adults, children also speak in different ways. The question is whether these two things go together; is there a link between the child's ways of understanding and speaking and his ways of thinking?

Chapter 1 described how the child's early attempts to communicate via language depend upon his ways of thinking. Before he can use words he has to be able to group things together that have something in common; the fact that he uses the word 'dog' to refer to all animals shows that he groups things that he feels share some common feature; the fact that he asks for milk when he wants some more suggests he knows that things still exist when they cannot be seen. The two word stage described in chapter 2 also reflects some of his ways of thinking. If we are right in thinking that 'Daddy coming' means something like 'Daddy is coming', he needs to have the idea that there is a link between a person who does an action and the action itself. So 'mine biscuit' suggests he has the idea of possession, 'here book' the idea of location. What is more, the fact that he combines words together to get 'another one artichoke' or 'mirrors on this knee' shows that he has grasped that things can be combined. Arranging bricks in a pattern may reflect the same general idea as arranging words in a sentence.

By the age of seven it is more uncertain how thinking affects language. Piaget has claimed that there is an important change in the child's system of thinking at about this age. This is when the child is first able to succeed in experiments like those with the glasses. According to Piaget the child now starts to use more mature ways of thinking called 'concrete operations', which means that he is no longer ruled just by the way things look, as was the child with the glasses. This change to a new type of thinking has some links with language development. Children who have made this change tend to describe things slightly differently from those who haven't. Shown two pencils of different sizes the child who has not made the change would typically say 'That one's thin and that one is a bit big' while the child who has made the change says 'That one is fatter than that one'. One tends to use two sentences joined by 'and', the other a single sentence comparing the objects mentioned. The next important stage in the child's mental development occurs in his teens and this will be discussed in chapter 6.

Thus there seem to be some links between language and general systems of thinking. A stage in mental development can correspond to a particular kind of language in the child. But this does not mean that one causes the other – that language leads to thinking. People have indeed tried to influence the child's system of thinking by teaching him the language that goes with the next stage of development. However, at the moment it is still an open question whether this makes any difference.

So adults have passed through the various stages of mental development without really being aware of it. They now think in very different ways from when they were younger. It is not just that children are trying to think in the same ways as adults but are not so good at it. Rather they have their own ways of thinking. The same is true of language. It is not that the child has failed to grasp some aspect of the meaning of a word, it is that the whole meaning may be different.

If language is so closely linked to thinking, the consequence may be that people who speak different languages think differently; a speaker of English thinks English thoughts – a speaker of Japanese, Japanese thoughts. For instance, speakers of English have no trouble deciding when to say 'I went to London' and when to say 'I have been to London.' It seems natural to use 'went to' about a particular moment in the past and 'have been to' when thinking of all the time before the present moment, so natural that it is hard to put the difference between them into words. A foreigner finds great difficulty in deciding which to use and continues to make mistakes, even if his English is otherwise very good. Though there could be several reasons for this, one possibility is that the idea that English speakers convey with 'have been to' is something peculiarly English. The fact that a person has learned English has influenced his ways of thinking in all sorts of subtle ways. Take for instance the way that languages describe things. In English the adjective usually comes before the noun, as in 'a red book' or 'cool beer' in which 'red' and 'cool' come before the nouns 'book' and 'beer'. In other languages such as French and Spanish the adjective usually comes after the noun. This might seem a trivial difference that would not really influence the way that people think. However when, in an experiment, English people were asked to put things into groups, they tended to do so first by putting things together that could be described by the same adjective, and only as a second thought those that could be described by the same noun. They put all the red things together first rather than all the things that were triangles. People who spoke the other kind of language did the opposite, first putting together all the triangles, then all the things that were red. The order of words in their own languages has made people sort things out differently, to see things with a slightly different emphasis. Of course this is only a small example and the effects of language on thinking should not be exaggerated. Speakers of human languages probably have more in common than they sometimes like to admit. Nevertheless it shows how learning a particular language can bias us towards thinking in a particular way.

At this general level there are then several links between language and systems of thinking. But there are also more specific ways in which language is linked to thinking. One of these is memory. Adult memory uses language to a large extent. This will be discussed in more detail in chapter 6. The point that should be made here is that the child starts with a very limited memory capacity. A child, for instance, can only remember a list of one or two words while the adult can remember seven or eight. In itself this limited capacity can explain quite a lot of the child's language development. The reason for his slow progress from one word to two words to longer sentences may be that this depends on his memory expanding. His mistakes with the glasses and the rows of objects may also show that he cannot remember them rather than that he thinks about them in different ways. Memory is used in many ways in speaking and thinking and influences the development of both in the child.

There is one more link between language and thinking that has to be mentioned. This is how the child uses language to control his own actions. In the early stages thinking affects language rather than the other way round and it is difficult for the child to use language as a way of controlling his actions. Several experiments show that his actions are more governed by what he sees than by language. Parents are doomed to a losing battle when they try to get young children to do what they are told. However well he understands 'Don't go near the fire', the language may still have no influence over the child's actions.

To sum up this chapter, the child thinks in ways that are sometimes extremely different from those of the adult and his language often means things that are different from the adult's. As he grows up language becomes more involved in his ways of thinking, in his memory and in his actions. Much of this, however, is still an open question since there are several different theories about how the child's mind develops, let alone the links between language and thinking. It is foolish to insist either that he should always be taught language so that he can think, or always taught thinking so that he can speak. Because of the different links between language and thinking and the ways in which these change as the child grows older, he needs to be taught both. Perhaps one day everything will be known about the relationship of language and thinking and definite advice can be given. At the moment it can safely be said that we ignore either of them at our peril. To come back to the example of the teacher and the bricks, the child has to be given the chance both to sort the bricks out in various ways and to use the language that goes along with this sorting.

5

The different kinds of English

So far this book has treated the English language as if it never varied. However, in reality there are many different kinds of English. Our language varies according to where we come from, what we are talking about, and in other ways. This chapter looks at some of these kinds and sees how they are linked to the child's language development.

One way of approaching the different kinds of English is to compare language with clothing. People in Britain by and large tend to wear the same kinds of clothes – trousers, dresses, socks, and so on. But you can still tell a good deal about a person by his or her clothes for the obvious reason that people with similar life-styles tend to dress similarly. A long ethnic dress, a sports jacket, a blue suit, a pair of jeans, all tend to give away something about the speaker's background. The same with the English language; a person's speech gives away something about them. If a strange voice on the phone asks 'Is Peter there?', you can probably guess the background of the caller just from these three words. English speakers are very good at spotting these clues in people's speech even if they can't say how they do it. The reason is that English varies from one place to another and from one social group to another. While the most obvious clues are accents, there are also particular ways of organizing sentences or particular words that can be as revealing. For instance I say 'I'm shrammed' when I feel very cold and this betrays that I lived in Wiltshire as a child. Each individual reflects the area he came from and the circumstances in which he was brought up.

Not surprisingly the child learns to speak the kind of English that he hears around him. If he hears an East London kind of English he learns to pronounce 'three' as 'free' and 'butter' as 'bu'er'; if he lives in the South of England with a middle-class background he thinks 'dinner' is in the evening rather than the middle of the day (except of course on Sundays and Christmas Day!); if he comes from America he talks about a 'sidewalk', from Britain a 'pavement'. It is unlikely that the child will learn a kind of English that is not used by the people he meets. At first he learns the kind of English spoken by his parents, later on by friends and acquaintances; generally speaking he talks like the people around him.

Does it then matter which kind of English the child learns? If he speaks a Glasgow kind of English? A Californian kind of English? A West Indian kind of English? An inner-city kind of English? In strictly logical terms of course it does not matter; jeans are just as effective as a suit at keeping legs warm and dry. There are undoubtedly differences between these kinds of English but difference does not necessarily imply inferiority, as the campaigners for women's and gay rights have pointed out. A city accountant dresses differently and uses different language from a Scottish miner but this does not mean that one is better than the other; the accountant's suit would be as out of place down a mine as a safety helmet in an office. No one seriously suggests that the accountant should adopt the customs and language of the miner. But of course some people have virtually suggested the reverse – that the miner or the miner's children should speak like the accountant. In other words they have felt that one kind of English is better than the others and have tried to get children to speak a kind of language that is not the one they hear around them. Is this in fact defensible? Are there valid reasons why some types of language are better than others and therefore to be fostered in children? The answer is complicated since language has many sides.

So far this chapter has pointed out that there are special kinds of English spoken in different regions and by different social groups. But in many parts of the world where English is spoken there is a particular kind that is not confined to a certain region but is spoken widely by members of a certain social group; this can be called the 'standard' kind of English.

Usually this is spoken by 'educated' people and hence is associated with certain classes, professions and levels of income; a person who has been to university is likely to speak it and so is a doctor or a lawyer. It is also found in schools and in the written language of most books and newspapers. It is more a matter of vocabulary and of the ways in which sentences are organized than it is of accent; in England people from many parts of the country speak standard English with a regional accent. On the one hand there is the difference between people's accents, which is fairly superficial, and on the other the difference between standard English and other kinds, which goes rather deeper.

Let us see then what case can be put forward for considering one kind of English superior to the others. One reason might be that it is more beautiful. But beauty is in the eye of the beholder; my wife thinks Elizabeth Taylor is more beautiful than Marilyn Monroe, Gregory Peck than Paul Newman, while I say the opposite. It is all a matter of taste. People may agree that some languages are more beautiful than others; English people often prefer Italian to German. But so far as different kinds of English are concerned, the ones which people seem to find most pleasing are either spoken by the better-off, more educated members of the community or by those who come from remote country districts. It is to say the least an odd coincidence that nobody enthuses about the beauty of the English spoken by industrial workers in large cities. The kind of English that sounds best to one's ears is that of the social group that has the most prestige; BBC is preferred to Birmingham, Boston to Brooklyn. There is no case for saying that a particular kind of language is beautiful without taking into account the ideas that people have of its speakers.

Another possible reason might be that more people can understand standard English than the other kinds. If you speak it you will be understood anywhere in the world where that standard is used and probably in other areas as well. The English of Swansea or of Chicago may be understood less readily outside the region where it is spoken. For this reason foreigners are usually taught standard English so that they will be able to get by wherever they go. But it is easy to overstate the problems of understanding non-standard kinds of English; most of them seem to pose little problem after the initial period of adjustment. In addition difficulties of understanding are often a matter of life-style rather than language. I remember hearing an American in a London theatre bar asking for 'A Scotch and a whisky', to the barmaid's total confusion. Her difficulty was caused as much by what drinks are normally available in England and America as by the difference between British English and American English; in the one Scotch whisky is usual, in the other rye. But a regional kind of language usually only becomes a handicap outside the region where it is spoken. Those who move from one district to another all the time or have no preference for one district rather than another, such as foreigners, may have to be more wary of speaking a regional kind than the rest of us who move only a few times in a lifetime.

But the reason for the superiority of one kind of language that is probably at the back of most people's minds is that it is more efficient at communicating than others. Hence they feel that those who do not speak standard English are less able to express themselves and that a child who says 'I didn't do nothing to nobody' is communicating less efficiently than one who says 'I didn't do anything to anyone.' So in the United States it was believed that Black Americans communicated less well than standard speakers and in England the same charge was made against the kinds of English spoken by West Indians and working-class people. The next step was to suggest teaching the child standard English so that he is not held back by his inefficient means of communication. It is obviously true that many members of these groups use kinds of English that differ from the standard. A black American may say 'That good' rather than 'That's good', a West Indian 'Make me go' rather than 'Let me go', a working-class child 'We was here' rather than 'We were here'. But all of these communicate perfectly efficiently to people who speak the same kind of English. They are different but this does not mean that they are inferior. Nor does it mean that the speakers of these kinds think any less logically than speakers of the standard kind. For the charge was often extended to say not just that these kinds were poor at communication but that they were inefficient for thinking as well; 'I didn't do nothing to nobody' or 'That good' were held to be not only inefficient but also illogical. But, though the last chapter suggested that people who speak different languages also to some extent think differently, who is to say which is best? The French, the Japanese, the Russians, would all claim that theirs was the best language for thinking. And the same applies to different kinds of the same language. The only reason that we think of one kind as better for thinking is that we associate it with certain kinds of people. It is even more dangerous to count on teaching the standard language to children as a way of teaching them to think. As was said in the last chapter, it is debatable whether teaching language can teach thinking; at best this may be true of certain aspects of thinking for certain age-groups. Why then is there a common impression that children who do not speak standard English do less well at school?

One simple answer is that standard English is used in schools. Children who already speak standard English naturally do better on tests that use standard English than children who speak other kinds. To put it in its most extreme form, a French-speaking child would score zero on a test given in English. What these tests often measure is the difference between the child's English and standard English rather than his educational achievements. Working-class children are handicapped to some extent because they are not familiar with the standard English used in schools and West Indian children may be even more handicapped because they are less familiar with the standard English used in Britain. If the children were tested in their own kinds of English, it is unlikely that the differences would be so great; if they were also taught in their own kinds, the differences might disappear. The disadvantage that these children have in the educational system, and ultimately in society at large, is mainly due to the emphasis that is placed on standard English, and the life-style that goes with it, rather than anything intrinsically wrong with their own kinds of English or their life-styles. There are, nevertheless, some people who speculate that certain types of language or life-style are an educational handicap in themselves rather than being different but there is still no solid evidence to prove this. The question arising from this is whether some children are 'deprived' of language; this is discussed in chapter 8.

The conclusion to be drawn from these arguments is that there is no real case for considering one kind of language better than another. But many people are left feeling rather uncomfortable by this. And of course they are right; the arguments above were purely in terms of language. Once you start looking at this issue from a wider perspective, you find other arguments to weigh in the balance. Language is part of the structure of our society and of our mental attitudes; we identify different kinds of language with different social groups and we have prejudices and preconceptions about it that affect us profoundly, even though they may be absurd when considered objectively. However equal standard English may be in terms of language, it is unequal in social terms. If a child is to do well in our present educational system, he will need to know standard English because his teachers will use it, his textbooks will be written in it, and his essays will be marked down if he does not use it; this is not to say that he has to forsake his own kind of English but that certainly within the school he has to be able to use the standard as well. If a person wants to follow a career such as accountancy or the law he or she also needs standard English and very often a particular accent as well. In some ways we need a language liberation movement to assert the rights of the different kinds of English. It is not that there is necessarily anything wrong with non-standard kinds; it is simply that people expect standard language to be used in certain circumstances and are annoyed or disconcerted if they do not find it. It is interesting for instance to notice what kinds of English are used in television commercials; rural accents of English are used only for advertising 'old-fashioned' traditional country foods such as sausages or cider; working-class town accents are either for comic housewives or for cartoon characters. Again the analogy with sexual or racial stereotypes is no accident: non-standard kinds of English are persistently shown as inferior. There is tremendous social pressure towards the standard. However much one may regret it, as a parent one has to take into account that one's children are going to have to fit into our society as it is today and that in many ways our society sets a particular value on standard English. It is certainly time for schools to question whether they should insist on the standard kind or instead try to accommodate the different kinds of English spoken by their pupils but teachers are members of the same society as everybody else and hence are likely to set the same store by the standard language. Indeed part of the handicap of the child who does not speak standard English may be, not that his language is different nor that he is not used to the school situation, but that the teacher expects him to do less well. In an ideal world all kinds of English would be equal; there is no intrinsic reason for saying one kind is better than any other. But in the real world certain kinds of English are spoken by social groups that have more status than others and one would be foolish not to equip one's child with the kind of English of the social group that one wishes him to belong to. But, of course, this is easier said than done.

For changing people's language can cut rather deeper than you might suspect. Both adults and children like to feel themselves part of a group; they like to belong somewhere. One way of showing which group you belong to is to speak its kind of language; using the group's language is putting on its uniform. It is possible that there are some differences between adults and children in loyalty to particular groups. An adult thinks of himself as a Yorkshireman or a Canadian even if he has been living in Manchester for the past thirty years; some traces of his origin will probably proclaim this still in his speech. A child is more flexible; my daughter Nicola changed her accent from East London to North London in a matter of months after we moved house; she adapted herself to the group in the new school she went to. One's sense of identity is closely bound up with the kind of language one speaks. The mildest comment on someone's language can be taken as a personal affront. So trying to change the kind of language that the child is using may suggest to him that you are attacking his identity and the group of which he is a member, perhaps his family or the children he knows or some other group. Whatever its effects on the child's language, a deliberate attempt to change the child's language to a form that you consider better does him more harm than good if it suggests you are rejecting the child's identity as part of a group. This is a special problem when the person who is correcting the child is not completely familiar with the kind of English he speaks. With West Indian children for example, a non-West Indian may find it hard to know which of the child's sentences are 'mistakes' and which are a different kind of English. Hence in a playgroup or school it is easy to seem to reject the child's own group. While there may be social reasons for encouraging standard English in the classroom, this must not be seen as an implied criticism of the child's background. The child should feel that the standard form is an alternative which is appropriate to certain circumstances but which does not threaten him in any way. By learning to use standard English he is adding something to himself rather than subtracting.

So far the kinds of English that have been discussed all differ between individuals; each person has a particular kind of their own that reflects their origin and social class – the groups to which they belong. However, the language of a single individual also varies according to the person he is talking to, where he is talking, what he is talking about, and other factors. Suppose you hear a man say on different occasions 'Bye-bye darling', 'Thank you, sir,' and 'That's all for now, Miss Jones.' You can tell from the language the relationships that he has with the people he talks to; 'darling' is different from 'sir' and different from 'Miss Jones'.

Once again it is helpful to compare language with clothes. People dress in different ways according to whether they are going to work or to church; they dress differently for different kinds of jobs; they wear pyjamas for going to bed, a raincoat for going out. The same with language; we change our language to suit the particular circumstances.

Or at least adults do. In the early years the child does not have a great variety of language addressed to him. Adults tend to adopt the same ways of speaking to children. Though there are other kinds going on around him, the language directed at him is fairly uniform. Nevertheless the child already from the beginning makes some changes according to the reason why he is using language; he distinguishes for instance between words for greeting and for playing. Another change that he learns to make is to whisper while his parents are on the phone or when he is too shy to speak to a stranger directly. But the child does not really develop this ability to switch from one kind of language to another till the school years. Some people believe that middle-class children are better at making these switches but once again one has to remember the handicap placed on children who speak non-standard kinds of English when they are put in an unfamiliar situation that requires the standard language. To generalize, probably a child who is used to using language in different ways finds it easier to adapt to the demands of a new situation, regardless of what class he comes from.

One distinctive kind of language that the child encounters at school is written language. Written English differs from spoken English in several ways. The types of sentence for instance are different; think of somebody saying 'SUMMER HOLIDAYS IN MADEIRA £30 off all July departures' or 'Tory plan "blueprint for industrial civil war" ', both taken from a newspaper, or even 'Mason was escorted into an office where the stale, close air gave forth that peculiar smell which clings to an office which is customarily occupied for twenty-four hours a day', taken from a detective story. Yet these are normal written English typical of their sources. To go a step further, some written documents such as contracts or prescriptions need an expert to interpret them to us. Without going into the controversies about learning to read, it is clear that in some respects written English is different from spoken English. A child who has some familiarity with this kind of English is more likely to become a fluent reader than one who has never met it before. And also of course written English tends to be standard English: once again children who speak non-standard kinds of English because of their class or regional background have an additional hurdle to surmount.

The child gradually learns this ability to handle different kinds of English. Indeed this goes on for the rest of one's life. There is always the possibility that one will find oneself in a situation that requires a kind of English one has never used before – an after-dinner speech, an appearance as a witness in court, a letter of complaint to the local newspaper. All these need their special kind of English. As children grow up they have to learn more and more of these specialized kinds of language for different occasions and for talking to different people.

One kind of English that is distinctive and that may have a particular importance in the early stages of learning to talk is the kind that adults use with young children – 'baby-talk' in other words. One of its distinctive qualities is its pronunciation; adults, for instance, tend to use a higher pitch when talking to children. But it is also a matter of 'baby-talk' words such as 'bow-wow' and 'wee-wee' which usually repeat the same syllable twice with little or no variation. However, much of the distinctiveness of language addressed to children is not so much *what* words are used as how often they are used. In terms of the types of sentence, children tend to be addressed far more questions to which the adult knows the answer than do adults. 'What colour's that, Jimmy?' is a question to which the speaker already knows the answer and would be strange addressed to an adult. But there's nothing strange about it being said to a child. Often the cause of the adult using particular forms to children more often than to adults is that he wants to simplify what he says to the child's level. He guesses what types of sentence the child can understand and adapts his own speech accordingly. All in all there is a special kind of language for talking to young children which is not just a matter of using special words. This kind of language in fact is common to parents everywhere, not just to those who speak English. It seems possible that this 'simplified' form of language actually helps the child to learn to speak. However there is no proof that this is so; strictly speaking one can say that 'baby-talk' is often used by adults to small children but one can not say whether this helps or hinders the child's development.

It is not surprising, since the child hears so much of it, that he picks baby-talk up quite easily. His own speech has many of the same characteristics; it too is 'simplified' and has special words. However, like the chicken and the egg, it is not certain which came first; it's impossible to tell if baby-talk by adults imitates children's speech or if children imitate adult's baby-talk. Nevertheless it is one of the first kinds that the child seems to recognize. Already between $3\frac{1}{2}$ and $4\frac{1}{2}$ children start to switch to something like baby-talk when they speak to young children rather than adults; they use simplified sentences, special baby-talk words, and special kinds of questions to babies but not to adults.

6

Language development after five

The earlier chapters of this book have already from time to time had to mention various aspects of the child's development after the age of five. For children do not suddenly become adult speakers at a particular age. Their language continues to change and develop until they are well into their teens. Indeed in some respects we are all still developing new ways of using language to fit changing circumstances. Language development after five may be less spectacular but there is still a considerable amount that the child has to learn. One important aspect is learning to read and write. Some people consider that this is *the* important aspect since it is the child's first step towards dealing with abstract things away from concrete situations. Other than drawing attention to its importance little will be said about it here since it goes well outside the limits of this book. A list on page 79 suggests some books on reading for those who are interested.

In some ways the child's development after five is not so much learning new things as doing old things better. He starts to lose the idiosyncratic features of his speech; my son for instance stopped saying 'Be be good' and 'railway lions'. He also stops using his own made-up past tenses such as 'comed' and 'goed'. The last remaining sounds that give him difficulty are learnt, usually the 'th' sounds in 'think' and 'father' and the sound spelled 's' in 'pleasure'. The child is filling in the gaps in his knowledge. He is also extending his range by using more kinds of language. One of these is the language used in the school classroom. Teachers use a particular kind of English in the classroom and expect their pupils to pick it up. Though chapter 5 drew attention to the importance of standard English in the school, it is true that classroom English has peculiarities of its own. For instance it is rather unusual in any other situation for one person to take sole charge of the conversation. Yet it is the rule in the classroom that the teacher always has control of the conversation, even to the extent of saying who is to speak next. In recent years it has become clear how different classroom English is from other kinds and the extent to which the child has to cope with a new kind of English in school. In most conversations, for instance, questions and answers form a pair:

'Have you read *Wuthering Heights*?'
'Yes, I liked it very much.'

In a classroom, though a question is followed by an answer, that answer is followed by a confirmation from the teacher as to whether it was right or wrong:

'What's three sevens, John?'
'Twenty-one.'
'Good'.

Instead of being a pair of question and answer it's a trio of question, answer, and confirmation. The reason is that teachers usually know the answers to their questions; what interests them is whether the pupil knows the answer too. In some ways then this is like parents talking to children.

As well as improving his performance of what he already knows, the child also learns some aspects of language for the first time after five. Take the ways in which the child understands and organizes sentences. By the age of five his sentences look very similar to those of adults and he seems to understand most of what is said to him. At first sight he has little more to learn in the way of organizing sentences. It is only when he is given a more searching test that some of the gaps in his language come to light. Chapter 3 described how the child first of all seems to use the normal English order of words in which the person who does something is mentioned first, then comes the verb, and the object or person that is affected by the verb is mentioned last. So in 'The postman brought a letter' the postman is the person who is doing something, the letter is the thing that was brought. By five the child has learnt that there are exceptions to this word in sentences such as 'A letter was brought by the postman' and 'Did the postman bring a letter?'; he knows how to deal with different word orders in the sentence. But there are still occasions when he is completely wrong. One of these is when he tries to understand sentences such as 'The man the dog bit was riding a horse.' If you ask him 'Who did the dog bite?' more often than not he will say 'The horse', not 'The man'. The reason for this is that these sentences are more complicated than they seem. 'The man the dog bit was riding a horse' could be split up into two sentences; 'The man was riding a horse' and 'The dog bit the man'. When these two are combined together the word order is deceptive. For, although 'a horse' comes after 'bit' in the sentence, the horse is not bitten, instead it is the man who is bitten even though he is mentioned first. The child does not realize this and so he uses his normal strategy that what comes after the verb is what is affected. He does not know that this sentence is a combination of two sentences, one inside the other, and that when you combine sentences together, odd things happen. This kind of sentence continues to give the child trouble in understanding even up to ten; indeed some adults get it wrong when they are given the same tests! Of course, testing a single point such as this taken away from a real language situation tends to paint a false picture of what the child can do. In a real situation he can use his common sense to help him to the right answer. Nevertheless wherever the child depends on how the sentence is organized, he still has a lot to learn.

Much of what he has to learn has to do with this same point about combining sentences together. A pair of sentences that people have studied is 'John is eager to please' and 'John is easy to please', this pair is now so famous that I have even seen the second one written in chalk on a brick wall in North London. The intriguing thing about these two sentences is that they seem to be organized in the same way. However, if you stop to think for a moment, you realize that the first sentence 'John is eager to please' implies that John wants to please other people, the second sentence 'John is easy to please' implies that other people please John. The differences between these are that on the one hand the sentence 'John is eager' is combined with 'John pleases people', on the other hand 'John is easy' is combined with 'People please

John'. When these sentences are combined together into the two alternatives, although the order of words and the ways they are organized look the same, they mean something different. Until they are six or seven children do not realize this and think they are dealing with an ordinary sentence such as 'John pleases people'. So, if they are asked to demonstrate 'The duck is easy to bite' with puppets, they will show the duck biting a wolf rather than the wolf biting the duck. Again the underlying reason is that these simple-looking sentences are really combinations of more than one sentence. The ways they have been combined together produce the same word order with different meanings.

Apart from these sophisticated ways in which sentences can be combined into one, the other major development is in the role that language plays in the child's mind. Language helps us to organize our thinking in many ways; gradually the child starts to use language in his thinking in the same ways as the adult. One example of this is word associations. We have all played word-games in which you are given a word and have to say the first word that comes into your head; someone says 'peaches' and you instantly reply 'apples'. The quickness of this reply shows that somewhere in your mind you have a connection between the word 'peaches' and the word 'apples'. But there is at least one important difference between the kinds of association given by children and by adults. This is the type of word that they give as an association. If you say 'blue' to a child, he is likely to say 'sky'; if you say 'blue' to an adult, he is likely to say 'red', or to give another colour. In the child's case he makes the word go together with another word, 'blue sky'. In the case of the adult he gives an alternative word that could be used instead of the first one, 'red' rather than 'blue'. The child tries to make the words hang together as if they were part of a sentence; the adult to give an alternative word from the same area. The child connects, the adult groups. The child gradually adopts the adult's way of associating till by his teens he is almost like the adult. However, it is still possible to get adults to give associations that connect words together like the child if you give them unusual words like 'obese' rather than common ones like 'blue'. For a long time then the child is using the same words as the adult but they do not mean the same to him because the associations, the links between them in his mind, are different. This is also shown in an experiment in which people are asked to remember long lists of words. The words belong to certain groups, say, names of flowers, vegetables, parts of the body, and so on. The lists, however, jumble the different groups up. But people who hear these lists do not remember them as jumbled up. Instead they tend to write down the words they remember group by group — they put 'rose' with 'tulip', 'sheep' with 'lamb'. Children on the other hand tend to put things together that have some kind of relationship between them — 'chair' goes with 'sit', 'bird' with 'fly'. Again the adult seems to group things, the child to connect them.

In these cases the child's way of using language slowly changes into the adult's. But with some aspects of memory it is not so much that the child changes as he comes to see the value of language for memory. Nor is it that he can just remember less than the adult, crucial as this may be to some aspects of language development. Rather his memory does not make nearly so much use of language. For instance, if an adult is trying to remember something for a few seconds, he remembers it in terms of the sounds of words. Shown a picture of a cat, he remembers the sounds of the word 'cat' even if no one actually says it. But up to the age of five or six children remember things more in terms of shapes or colours rather than sounds. If they are shown a picture of a cat, they remember a black furry animal rather than the word 'cat'. So children under six tend to muddle things in their memory that look alike, adults to muddle things whose names sound alike.

This brings us back to the links between language and thinking. Though it is difficult to say exactly where one begins and the other ends, one can nevertheless try to see how much certain types of thinking rely on language. Thus using sounds to remember things is one way of using language. Another is to put labels on things, to give them names. Almost without being aware of it, adults put mental labels on what they have to remember because they find that this helps them. If they are shown a card with a colour on it, they are more likely to remember it by the labels 'blue-gray' or 'salmon-pink' than by the colour itself. Children of five, however, don't use labels in this way; they remember the colour rather than the word. As they get older, they start labelling more and more. It isn't so much that the child of five is incapable of using labels to help his memory; indeed he will do so quite happily if asked. Rather he does not see the advantages of labelling. Once again, the older the child gets, the more useful he finds language in his thinking.

Indeed by the teens language and thinking in some ways seem to have become one. Unfortunately little research has been carried out on the language of this age-group. It seems likely that the child now attains a new level of thinking in which he can reason abstractly without being limited to the properties of actual objects – what Piaget calls the level of 'formal operations'. He can work out hypothetical ideas that he knows are false – what would happen if the moon landed in the Pacific Ocean? The development towards abstract thinking that started with learning to read has reached its culmination. But, while it is clear that language is closely involved in this kind of thinking, it is far from clear just how it is involved.

To sum up, there are still many aspects of language development after the age of five about which little is known. Certainly the child is still learning new ways of organizing sentences, particularly the ways in which they can be combined together. He is also evidently learning to integrate language with the other processes going on in his mind. By his teens he is using language for abstract thinking and it is well-nigh impossible to say any longer which is language and which is thinking.

7

Helping the under-fives with language

Time and again this book has stressed that there are many sides to language development. This means that there are also many different ways of helping the child's language. Chapter 1 described four main reasons for using language – interacting with people, communicating, thinking, and playing. Helping the child may therefore mean helping him to interact with others, to communicate with them, to organize his ideas, and to play with language. When talking of helping the child it is all too easy to forget these different aspects of language and to concentrate on narrow aspects of vocabulary or the organization of sentences to the neglect of the other ways in which the child can be helped.

The most important guideline in helping children is the most obvious: talk to them. Though there is still controversy about the precise ways in which children can be helped, it seems certain that the child needs as much talk as he can get. This is not to say that he should simply be exposed to language, that the radio or television should be left permanently on in the background. Talking is a two-way process of give and take; though one person talks and the other listens, the speaker is continually adapting what he is saying to the listener's reactions and the listener usually has the right to take over and start speaking himself when he feels like it. But whatever the child's reactions the person on television does not alter what he is saying, nor can the child butt in. Talking to children means taking part in conversations with children and in a conversation the speaker has the constant duty to see that the listener can follow what he says and to adapt himself to the listener's reactions rather than riding over him roughshod. Even quite simple changes in the amount of conversation can have quite dramatic effects on the child. Three psychologists, for instance, were asked to help a $3\frac{1}{2}$-year-old whose language was backward and who used only a few words. They suggested that the mother should ask the child to repeat words more often and that she should speak to him more. The leap forward this produced in the child's language was quite surprising.

If the adult is talking naturally to the child, he will be adapting his language to the child's language level and his reactions. At its most obvious this amounts to baby-talk — adults speaking to children make their sentences simpler, they ask more questions, they use a higher pitch, and so on. However, nobody has proved that baby-talk actually helps children to learn to speak. But there are many other ways in which the adult adapts his speech to the needs of a child listener who has a different range of interests from himself, some of them subtle and very complicated to describe. It would be possible to give a list of instructions on how to talk to children but this list would be long and very technical. One instruction might be 'Avoid sentences that are combinations of more than one sentence'. This is a lot easier to say than to do. But there seems very little point to this list since all it does is reflect the automatic ways that adults modify their speech when talking to children in any case. Talking to children makes an adult talk in a particular way if he is genuinely trying to have a conversation and there is no need for him to be consciously aware of the subtle adaptations he is making to his normal speech. Indeed a conscious awareness of this may stifle the conversation.

This is not to say that anything an adult says to a child is automatically perfect. For there is an important difference to be made between talking *to* children and talking *at* children. Talking *to* children means a two-sided conversation in which the child's point of view is as good as the adult's. At one moment the adult may be speaking; the next the child may take over the role of speaker. Both of them are continually adapting what they are saying to the other person's reactions. Because of this the speaker usually tries to say something that is relevant and interesting to the listener and changes tack if the listener shows the wrong reaction. Talking *at* children means a one-sided conversation where the adult dominates and controls everything that goes on. He is only concerned with getting his point of view over, not with the other person's point of view. There are many ways in which conversation with children can become talking *at* rather than *to*. One is when the adult asks questions to which he already knows the answer – 'What colour's that, Jimmy?' when Jimmy knows perfectly well that the questioner knows what colour it is and is just checking whether the child knows too. Another way is to use language to control what they are doing 'Wipe your shoes,' 'Don't touch that,' 'That isn't the book you want, is it?' A third way is to give a stream of information, whether to the baby in the pram or the child being taken round a museum. All of these present the adult in a single role – the dominant person who is entitled to overrule anything the child feels or wants to say. In an absolute sense there may be nothing wrong with this; the children of Victorian parents learnt to speak just as well as anybody else though they were in this kind of situation. In other parts of the world children manage to learn to speak even when adults regard it as beneath them to talk to children. Nevertheless one of the causes of handicap in children in our educational system is often claimed to be that some social backgrounds do not allow the child to use language in a variety of ways, not just as the passive recipient of the adult's speech. One piece of evidence for this comes from some research which compared two types of residential nursery and two types of language. In one type of nursery the organizer is very much in charge and the assistants follow a routine that is carefully laid down for them; the language here tends to be talking *at*. In the second type of nursery the assistants are much more free to use their own initiative and have responsibilities of their own; the language here tends to be talking *to*. It was found that the children in the second type who were talked *to* were more advanced at language than those in the first type. Children did better in the situation where they were treated more flexibly, both in terms of the organization of the nursery and in terms of language.

The other reason why it is beneficial to talk to children goes back to the discussion of the different kinds of English in chapter 5. There it was suggested that in our society a child is handicapped to some extent if he cannot switch from one kind of language to another, in particular from the non-standard kind to the standard kind in certain situations. The child needs to experience different kinds of language if he is to be able to use them himself. Talking *at* people is only one kind of language, where the child always has to play the subordinate role and the adult orders him about, asks him rhetorical questions, and deluges him with information. Talking *to* people embraces a variety of rules, not just the adult authority versus the helpless infant. Listen to a playgroup supervisor talking *at* the children – 'Come here, Sylvia.' 'Don't touch, you'll break it.' 'You're baking a cake – very good.' 'I'm going to put the stick away.' This language is vital to running a playgroup. But if it's the chief kind the child hears it will not extend his language. Listen to another supervisor sitting at a table with some children playing with playdough – 'It smells like bread?' 'Shall we make something?' 'Are you going to make something with us?' 'Do you remember when we ...?' This supervisor is joining in the conversation as an equal, not as a superior, using 'we' and 'us' rather than 'you', talking about her own sensations, reminding them of their common experiences. Though she is still guiding them in particular directions, she is not doing so by asserting the adult's right to dominate children. The very fact that she is sitting beside the children and playing with playdough herself helps her adopt this role.

So the second important thing is to use different kinds of language. Unless they hear a variety of kinds of English, they will not learn to use language in the ways that are available to the adult. One kind of difference is in terms of the roles that people take up in conversation; a constant superior-to-inferior kind of language prevents the child from learning to use other kinds. But there are many other different kinds of language. The child should be starting to explore the different reasons for using language. He should be encountering different regional and social kinds of English. He should be seeing how one person's language can vary according to who they are speaking to and so on. He should also be meeting the difference between spoken language and the written language of books. It is the richness of his language experience that counts.

Rather than think of particular activities to help children's language it is more useful to think of the general principles of talking to them and giving them a rich experience of different kinds of language. These general principles have consequences for the activities that are used with under-fives. Particular activities arise out of children's individual needs and interests and, without knowing the individual child, one can only suggest general guidelines. At this moment for instance my son Robert is writing a letter to the Dennis the Menace Fan Club, asking us to spell each word that he wants to write.

This activity comes out of his own interests and seems a useful way for him to approach writing. But it would be highly dangerous to recommend this as an activity for all children learning to write. The other reason for concentrating on general principles is that there is the risk, once one starts describing particular activities, not to see the wood for the trees. It is easy to be side-tracked into thinking up more and more ingenious things for children to do without considering *why* they should do them, of devising some new way of playing with water without relating it to the reasons for having water-play in the first place.

Furthermore the typical activity that people associate with language only concerns one side of language development. For instance, children are shown a number of objects about some particular theme, say clothes. They see people wearing jackets and boots, uniforms and hats, socks and dresses; an adult provides a running commentary – 'Isn't that a funny hat!', 'Look, he's wearing a kilt!' Then the children participate in the activity in one way or another; they sort clothes out into piles, they draw them and colour them, they dress up in them. This is the usual activity in many television programmes and books aimed at improving the language of the under-fives. There are many different ways of doing it but the thing that they all have in common is the idea that it is important for the child to name things and to put them into groups. I do not wish to suggest that there is not a valuable place for this in the child's life but the value may come more from the opportunity it provides for interacting with an interested adult or for the insight it gives the child into sorting things into groups than from the language. It was suggested in chapter 1 that naming was only one of the processes involved in language learning. Chapter 6 also pointed out that the child does not have the adult's automatic habit of labelling what he sees. Hence these activities concentrate on something that is only a single aspect of language learning and that in some ways is beyond his present way of thinking. Provided that these activities are not the only ones used with the child they can be a great help. But it is dangerous if the adult thinks that these are all he has to do to help the child's language. Instead there should be a mixture of activities that make use of different aspects of language.

Let us look now at some of the general approaches towards helping children's language. Before doing so, this is the place to point out that this chapter deals with normal language development rather than any of the things that can go wrong with it. If you suspect that a child has something wrong with his speech, you should contact a qualified speech therapist through a health centre or an educational welfare service. They have their own efficient ways of treating children from an early age onward.

Do not rely on the advice of people who are not specialists on children's language; people working with the health or education of young children have the best of intentions when they talk about the child's language but do not have the specialized knowledge and experience.

There are three general approaches towards helping normal language development. The first of these is to concentrate on language itself. The child is given practice in particular aspects of language, say, vocabulary or particular types of sentence. An adult might decide that a child needs help with sentences that describe where things are. He starts by showing the child a picture of a zoo and asks him questions about where the animals are – 'Where's the tiger? Where are the children?' Then he takes toy animals and puts them in various places around the room, getting the child to describe where they are. Finally he hides the animals in different places and the child has to find out where they are by asking him questions, or the child looks for them and has to come back and say where he found them. The aim of the activity is for the child to say and hear a number of sentences with the same pattern – 'The tiger's in the cage', 'The lion's under the chair.' This approach picks out one small point about language and gives intensive practice. Though the point illustrated here happened to be a particular way of organizing sentences, other aspects of language could have been chosen just as well. For instance if the child has difficulty with pronunciation he may be given practice on particular sounds; he can practice the 'sh' sound in 'fish' by having to say whether a picture shows a sheet or a seat or by repeating tongue twisters such as 'Sister Susy sewing shirts for sailors on the sea-shore.' The snag with this approach is that, to be used properly, it requires a fairly technical knowledge of the English language. Though it has been used for various language syllabuses, particularly for children who do not speak English as a mother tongue, this approach is not so popular among those concerned with the development of the first language. The reason for this is that it tends to concentrate on *how* the child speaks rather than *why* he speaks. There may be little point in teaching the child a particular aspect of language if he has no immediate need to use it. Practicing saying 'fish' may hardly affect his language if it does not come when he is actually asking for fish and chips. Of course at its best, this approach makes the language practice meaningful by integrating it with the child's activities, as in the example above. But many aspects of language do not lend themselves to this treatment, and have to be practiced in a more artificial way.

The second approach to helping children's language is to concentrate on communication rather than language itself – on, one of the reasons why the child uses language. The activities in this approach try to make the child communicate something to somebody else. He is not just telling things to people, he is seeing if they understand what he means. For instance, try asking a child to tell you how to draw an elephant and then follow exactly what he says. If he communicates effectively, the drawing should have the legs, trunks, tusks, and so on in the places that he means them to be. This is not to say of course that they will be in the places that the adult thinks they should be! The activity makes the child communicate something to the adult and helps him to see whether he has been successful, whether the other person has understood what he was trying to say. It does not make the child practice any particular aspect of language itself; instead it makes him try to communicate with whatever language he can summon up. This approach has been used chiefly by those who are trying to compensate for what they believe are gaps in some children's experience of language. An interesting collection of activities that use communication can be found in a book called *Talk Reform* by D. M. and G. A. Gahagan which describes an experiment that tried to compensate for possible deficiencies in the language experience of working-class children. In general, though this approach has a lot to be said for it in that it makes the children do something with language rather than simply practice language for its own sake, it is only part of the answer. Indeed its chief merit may be that it involves close interaction with adults or other children. Communication is only one of the reasons for language and some children have more need to practice language for forming relationships or for play than for communication.

The third approach relies on the links between language and other aspects of the child's development. Chapter 4 showed that there are various links between language and the child's ways of thinking, how much he can remember, and so on. In this approach language is improved indirectly by tackling the other aspects of development on which it is believed to depend. So, for instance, children are given things to sort out into piles of long and short, fat and thin, red and blue. From this they learn something about the idea of comparing things and they are equipped to learn the ways the English language has for expressing comparison – 'This one's bigger than that', 'My one's bigger than yours.' The children's language has been helped by giving them practice with a concept that is expressed through language. Language may be hindered by lack of development in other areas as well as concepts. The child may, for example, find it hard to understand or produce certain sentences because his memory is too small to cope with them, or the amount of attention he can give them is not enough. A book called *Helping language development* by J. Cooper, M. Moodley, and J. Reynell describes a programme of activities designed for use with children with language handicaps. In general the difficulty in this kind of approach is knowing what aspects of development contribute to language with any certainty.

All of these approaches then demand a great deal of knowledge and careful planning to devise particular activities that help language. Though it is useful to know something about them in principle, it is safer to leave the actual practice to the experts. What advice can one give in addition to the earlier suggestions? Rather than devising activities that are aimed directly at helping language, it is better to consider how language is involved in what the child is already doing. Often if one thinks of the language implications of the child's everyday activities, one finds ways in which language could be helped by making fairly minor changes. Take the Wendy House for instance. If you listen to children speaking in a Wendy House at a playgroup, you hear them say things such as 'You've got no blanket.' 'This is our bed.' 'Naughty girl, you're a naughty girl.' This is language being used for social relationships and it is obviously useful for the child to act out the kinds of family relationship with which he is familiar. However, the children's language is not being extended. The language comes from an area which they already know well. Suppose, however, that the Wendy House is turned into a hospital for the morning. Without doing any more, a whole new kind of language has been introduced. The roles of the children are now doctors, patients, radiologists, or ambulance drivers. They have to talk about different things – describe symptoms, prescribe treatment, reassure people. If the day when the Wendy House becomes a hospital is linked to a visit by the health visitor or to a real accident that one of the children has had, so much the better. Sometimes of course simply changing the function of the Wendy House is not enough to make the children start using the new language of the hospital situation. In this case an adult has to show them some of the new 'hospital' language, probably best done by taking part for a while in their game as doctor or patient. Another day the Wendy House could be a garage, another a police-station, depending on the children's interests. Changing the function of the Wendy House extends the kind of language that is used. The children's language is being helped because they are having to use it in a greater variety of roles and situations. This is not to say that the children will produce language that is anything like the real language of hospitals; rather it is their attempt at using language in a new way that is important.

Another common playgroup activity is called variously Great Circle, Newstime, or Grouptime. This is the activity in which all the children are gathered into a group and the supervisor discusses things with them – 'Anybody got any news?' 'Michael is trying to tell us something.' This often leads into a straightforward language activity – 'Do you know what a hippopotamus is?' 'Have *we* got eyebrows?' – and finishes with a counting activity, a ring-game, a song, or the distribution of milk.

Supervisors have claimed to me that the point of this activity is both language and encouraging the child to speak to a large group of people as he will have to do when he goes to school. But let us compare this kind of activity with what happens in ordinary life. Do we ever meet together in groups in this way to have guided discussions about news and views? The answer is that this is rather rare. Usually when we meet in groups it is as an audience, in which case all we do is clap our hands, or as a 'meeting' of a committee or group, in which case we are trying to decide something. It is rare that we would suddenly say to a group of twenty people 'I went to the cinema last night.' It may be natural for the supervisor to give out news and announcements in a Great Circle, as is done in a school assembly, but it is better to reserve discussion with the children to small groups, where the supervisor can follow their individual interests and needs more closely and make certain that all the children are contributing and paying attention. The Great Circle works better for activities that are naturally done in groups, receiving news from the supervisor or taking part in group activities such as ring-games and songs. So looking at the language involved in a Great Circle can make us decide to change its format.

The same is true of the various rhymes used in games and songs. A moment's thought about their language can help us to make them more effective language practice. Partly these rhymes are important because they bring in the idea of playing with language itself, one of the reasons for using language, whether it is for songs or for trying out strange noises like the animals in 'I had a cat and the cat pleased me' with their cries of 'chimmy chuck', 'swishy, swashy', and 'griffy, gruffy'. The repetition of sentences in this kind of rhyme also helps the child with any words or expressions he does not know. Indeed the way in which some nursery rhymes gradually build up sometimes gives the child examples of how sentences are combined together.

This is the house that Jack built.
This is the malt that lay in the house that Jack built.
This is the rat that ate the malt that lay in the house that Jack built.

This can show how the sentence may be made longer and longer by combining more sentences together. Perhaps more importantly these rhymes depend on particular ways of people interacting together, on particular 'routines'. At the early stages the rhymes that go down best are those with routines that involve actual physical contact. Some rhymes are accompanied by touching various parts of the child's head or his fingers and end with tickling such as:

> Round and round the garden
> Like a teddy bear
> One step, two steps,
> Tickle you under there

and

> Ring the bell,
> Knock at the door,
> Peer in,
> Lift the latch,
> Walk inside,
> Go way down cellar and eat apples.

These integrate the language and the action into a simple routine for adult and child. Later on games like 'The farmer's in his den' or 'Oranges and Lemons' have more complicated routines in which the children act and speak at the same time. Rhymes are also undoubtedly useful practice at the rhythms of speech and at recognizing whether two sounds are the same.

Nevertheless there has to be a certain amount of caution in choosing them. Many use rather old-fashioned language and are about things that children are unfamiliar with. What for instance is 'curds and whey'? What are children to make of 'ring-a ring-a roses', a song supposed to be about the symptoms of the plague? Though the main reason for using rhymes may be to play with language, this doesn't mean that they should be completely irrelevant to the children's lives. After learning carols at school last Christmas my son for instance was convinced that a little girl called Merrily lived in heaven ('Merrily on high') and that the king of Israel was called Born ('Born is the king of Israel').

Children try to make sense out of what they are saying; even a rhyme might as well mean something to them. Some primary-school teachers have said to me that children know more television commercials than nursery rhymes. The reason for this may be that commercials are about things that children know and understand, rhymes are often about strange things in an obscure kind of language. Even from the point of view of practising the rhythms of speech, care must be taken, for many rhymes use rhythms that are unusual in ordinary speech. If I read 'Jack and Jill went up the hill to fetch a pail of water' as an ordinary piece of prose I give it a quite different rhythm from the one I use when I am saying it as a nursery rhyme.

One can hardly leave the subject of helping children with language without mentioning books. From a language point of view one of the chief merits of books is that they provide a range of different kinds of English. In a book the child meets language used in all sorts of ways by all sorts of people. Partly this is a matter of familiarizing the child with the types of sentence and vocabulary found in written language. Take the opening of Snow-white and the Seven Dwarfs in the Brothers Grimm version:

> Once upon a time in the middle of winter, when the flakes of snow were falling like feathers from the sky, a queen sat sewing at a window framed in black ebony.

If you were telling the same story from memory it would be more like:

> Once upon a time there was a queen and this queen was sitting at a window sewing. The window-frame was made of black wood. Outside it was snowing very hard.

The spoken version simplifies the language by splitting the sentence up into several sentences, each organized in a simple way. The vocabulary also has changed. These changes not only take away part of the magic of the story, they make it more like spoken English. Written language can be more elaborate and have a powerful effect because the writer has the time to think and to prepare what he is writing. Spoken language can rarely be so prepared and controlled. Reading the child a story helps him to appreciate the rather different kind of English that is found in writing.

There are other kinds of language which are made available through books. Some use factual language for describing things:

> One of the buildings where people are busy at night is a newspaper office. Night editors are preparing news and pictures. (H. Kurth, *A Night in Town*)

Others show the language of poetic fantasy:

> Far beyond the jungles and the burning deserts lay the bright blue ocean that stretched forever in all directions. There were little green islands with undiscovered edges and whales swam round them in this sort of way. (M. Peake, *Captain Slaughterboard drops anchor*)

Others rely on down-to-earth situations, like the bus-conductor complaining to the Brick Street Gang 'If I see that ball again I'll jump on it and flatten it and chop it up into a thousand pieces.' (A. Ahlberg, *A Place to Play*). Books also show the child that people of different backgrounds speak differently whether it is the polite middle-class conversation of Topsy and Tim:

> 'I'm getting hungry,' Topsy whispered to Tim.
> 'Serves you right!' replied Tim who had eaten an enormous breakfast.'

(J. & G. Adamson, *Topsy and Tim visit the Tower of London*) or the earthy style of Raymond Briggs' *Father Christmas* with his 'Blooming Christmas here again!' and 'Fiddling buttons!' This diversity of English available in books serves to introduce the child to a range of different kinds of English. But it also serves to reassure him by showing him that his own kind of English is worthy of being in a book. For instance the Nipper series of readers took pains that the child would find his own word for 'mother' somewhere in the series; one book might have 'mummy', another 'ma', another 'mum', and so on. Rather than feeling that his own kind of English is something that is peculiar and that people disapprove of, by seeing it in a book he is reassured that it is as good as any other. Unfortunately while it is comparatively easy to find books for schools now that show a variety of groups with different kinds of language, it is still hard to find ones suitable for under-fives. There is some concession being made to having characters from different groups, races and sexes, but where are the books that actually use the language of, say, West Indians living in London? Books not only introduce the child to new kinds of language, they also reassure him about the status of his own language. Page 79 gives a short list of books that I have found useful from a language point of view.

There are of course limits to the kinds of English that are suitable for the child. In particular there needs to be some check that the books that are read to the child contain 'real' kinds that are useful to him. There is everything to be said for giving the child imaginative language that broadens his horizons. But there are dangers in giving him kinds of language that have no currency outside children's books. This specially applies to fairy stories where there is a temptation for the writer to use a deliberately quaint style of writing. Take a book like *The Three Bears* by William Stobbs. Charming as it is, the language is rather curious. Take the sentence 'One day, after they had made the porridge for their breakfast, and poured it into their porridge bowls, they walked out into the wood while the porridge was cooling, that they might not burn their mouths by beginning too soon to eat it.' The last part of this sentence has two odd things about it. First of all it is strange in modern English to say 'that they might not burn'; instead we would usually say 'so that they wouldn't burn'. 'That they might not' sounds rather like an old translation of the Bible. Secondly instead of saying 'by beginning too soon to eat it', we would usually say 'by beginning to eat it too soon'; the 'too soon' would normally come at the end rather than in the middle. This quaint language resembles no kind of English the child is likely to meet outside a fairy-tale, and does not seem useful to the child's language development. Nor does it seem sufficiently poetic to be worth using for its own sake, as a poem might be.

The other negative point to be made about choosing books to help under-fives is – be wary of books that are specially designed to teach reading. For the language in these has been chosen, quite rightly, to help the child to *read*, not to help him to *speak*. The ways in which it has been chosen reflect different methods for teaching children to read. Take a Ladybird book for instance which starts 'Here are Peter and Jane. They like to play. Up they go. Up, up, up they go. I like this, says Peter. It is fun.' However useful this may be as a way of teaching children to read, it doesn't seem likely to help their language to any great extent. For the idea of this kind of reading book is to keep the language simple and repetitive, so that the child has only a limited number of words and shapes to remember, and so that he can concentrate on learning to read without being confused by language he doesn't know. The language is deliberately within the child's limits rather than trying to stretch them. Another reading method, however, emphasizes the links between sounds and letters. A Dr Seuss book starts 'Up. Pup. Pup is up. Cup. Pup. Pup in cup.' The child's attention is drawn to the links between sounds and letters by varying one at a time – 'Up/pup/cup', 'in/is'. The language is specially chosen to reflect these links. So in both of these methods the language is distorted in different ways to help the child to read. Whatever their merits as reading schemes, there is nothing to recommend them for language work with under-fives. Of course there are other reasons why some of these books are read to under-fives; it would be a sad child who had never met the Cat in the Hat. But in general it is dangerous to choose books from reading schemes solely as a way of helping the child's language. One method for teaching reading does, however, use books that are based on the actual language of children after the initial stages of learning to read. This is the *Breakthrough to Literacy* series. *My Mum* for instance starts 'My mum. My mum is big. My mum is pretty. I go to school with my mum. After school I go home. I have tea with my mum.' But most books for teaching reading reflect neither normal written language nor the language that children actually hear or say.

Two other points can be made about using books with under-fives.

One is the vexed questions of teaching the child to read.

My own opinion is that this depends on the individual child. Some children are ready for reading and it is a shame to postpone giving them the pleasure of being able to read something themselves. But most children are probably not ready till they are at school and it may be harmful to try to make them read, particularly if the person who is teaching them does not know much about the methods of teaching reading or is blindly following a particular patent method. On the other hand, just sitting beside an adult as he or she reads teaches the child some important things about reading such as the way we turn pages from right to left, or the way we interpret pictures or read sentences from left to right and top to bottom, or the way that a story links events in a sequence. These are skills that need to be learnt and the child picks them up naturally by being read to. Children are also unlikely to want to read if they do not see other people reading. Why should they bother if their parents can get along perfectly well without reading? However much the parent may insist, their example counts for more. In my own case I realized that I happened to do most of my reading at night when the children never saw me. So I deliberately started sitting around with a book at a time when the children were still up.

The other point is that the activity of reading aloud to a child has a social function that is as important as the language. Taking part in the same experience as the adult, looking at the same pictures together, talking about the pictures and the story, these are ways in which the child is forming a relationship with the adult. Even in primary school the value of reading aloud to the teacher may be not so much the improvement in the child's reading as the opportunity for the teacher to pay close attention to just one child for at least one part of the day. A book like Raymond Briggs's *The Snowman* which has no words at all but consists of a series of pictures telling the story helps the child's language by giving him the chance to interact with an adult about a particular theme.

This chapter started with a reminder of the many reasons that we have for using language. Mostly it has concentrated on the the use of language for communicating, for interacting with people, and for playing. What about language for thinking? It was suggested in an earlier chapter that for the most part language depends upon thinking in the under-fives rather than thinking depending upon language. So there is not much point in devising language activities specially to help the child's thinking. This still leaves open the question of providing activities that directly help the child to develop his thinking but this is outside the scope of the present book. Essentially this chapter has concentrated on a few general principles for helping children rather than suggesting particular activities that should be used. There is still controversy about how one should help children's language, about how the facts about children's language development given in earlier chapters can be turned into practical advice on what one should or shouldn't do. It is hard to see, however, how it could ever be wrong to talk to children as individuals, or to give them a rich experience of different kinds of language. Nor can it be harmful to stop and think how these two general principles can be applied to the everyday activities that we share with children. The most important thing for language development is an adult with a genuine interest in the child and in what the child has to say.

8

Questions and Answers

The purpose of this chapter is to take some of the questions I am often asked about children's language and to answer them as reasonably as possible in the light of what is known about children's language today. Some of these answers look at things that have already been mentioned but from a slightly different angle. Others are about new topics. None of them are of course the final word. There are still many areas of children's language in which all too little is known, particularly how to help the child's development. There are also basic disagreements about various aspects of language; any answers to questions about helping children must be not only tentative but also controversial.

1 Is watching television good or bad for children's language?

First it is useful to put on one side the aspects of watching television that have nothing to do with language. It may or may not lead to increased violence or permissiveness; it may or may not be a boon to the schoolteacher; certainly it can be a boon to the parent coping with a tired and irritable child. The question is rather whether it helps or hinders the child's language.

To me the advantage of television is the different kinds of language that the child can meet. Any day he can see people from different parts of the world speaking different regional and social kinds of English; he sees people describing, arguing, or explaining; people in factories, in offices, in courts or in farms. The child is shown a range of different worlds, each with its own kind of language, far more than any home or playgroup could supply. The child escapes his own limited experience of language and hears it being used in all sorts of ways. Oddly enough this aspect is rarely developed in programmes aimed directly at under-fives. Mostly these have youngish presenters from a middle-class background using a studio set that is the same from week to week, not to mention decade to decade. The language that is used has a heavy 'educational' bias towards shapes, telling the time, and similar ideas. Its one distinctive quality is the way in which the presenters use a low pitch and break up their sentences with long pauses, not to mention the coy looks they give the camera. To give the child a useful range of English you need people of different ages, different classes and different regions, not only to expand the children's range, but also to reassure them of their own identity as part of a group by showing them speakers of their own kind of English. When did you last see live children speaking on a programme for under-fives, let alone old-age pensioners? The potential of television is that it can show adults and children doing a variety of things at home and at work, having all sorts of relationships with people and behaving in all sorts of ways. The most useful programmes for under-fives are not in my opinion those that are specially designed for them because these tend to be pale imitations of a class or playgroup situation. The children may get more out of an American mass-produced cartoon or a pop song in terms of meeting new kinds of language.

The snag though is that television is one-sided; it does not make the child take part. Most kinds of language involve a give-and-take between speaker and listener. The child can observe this give-and-take happening on the television but he never takes part in it himself. Where the object of the language is communication, to tell people things, this may not be so much of a handicap. But where language has other objects, television can only supply a model of what the child should do rather than actually getting him to do it. Learning language requires a close relationship with people – trying to say things to them, trying to interact with them. Television is a poor substitute for a real person. One way round this difficulty is to adapt the advice given during the water shortage – take a bath with a friend. In other words, watch television with an adult who can supply part of the missing give-and-take by discussing and asking questions about the programmes. Indeed a programme such as *Sesame Street* sets out to attract an adult audience as well as children so that there is someone for the child to share his experiences with.

2 What do I do in a playgroup with a child that does not speak English?

In many areas it is now common for a playgroup supervisor or nursery teacher to be faced with a child who speaks little or no English and it is a genuine problem knowing what to do. First of all, to repeat the point made in chapter 5, speaking a particular language or kind of language stamps you as a member of a particular group: French people speak French, Scottish people have a Scottish accent. Learning a new language means that this sense of identity with a group may be threatened; you may feel you are giving up part of yourself when you learn a foreign language. However much he consciously complains about his poor accent, an immigrant who identifies himself with his own country will never lose it. Changing from one language to another is in this respect an exaggerated case of changing from one kind of the same language to another. A child who speaks another language needs reassuring that his own language is still being valued even if people are trying to get him to use English. Somewhere within the school or the playgroup I feel there has to be something that the child can point to and say 'That's what *we* do'. In a school it might be nothing more than a few books in the library in Greek or Chinese, or whatever. Even if the child does not read them, he can still see that some value is put on his own language. In a playgroup it might be getting the child to tell a song or a rhyme in his own language, or to say what one or two things are called. Apart from helping the child himself, this can have a useful effect on the other children and on their parents.

What about the actual learning of English by the child? So far as children under five are concerned, the evidence at the moment suggests that they learn a second language in much the same way that they learnt a first. The stages of development are similar and the 'mistakes' that they make are like those made by native children, of course at a younger age. So the advice for handling children who speak another language is, broadly, to speak to them the same as to native children. Some people suggest a programme based on particular aspects of language, as described in chapter 7, but many feel that the important thing is simply to talk to the child as much as possible in as many ways as possible, adapting one's speech in the automatic ways one does for children and remembering that the child's level of English is way below his actual age. Do not worry if the child appears to use no English at all for some time; many children go through this phase in learning a second language. The soundest advice is that given by a teacher at the United Nations nursery school in Paris, which has to cope with forty-six nationalities: 'The best way to encourage the acquisition of a new language for the child is to have happy experiences with friendly persons in sympathetic surroundings, where the learning is spontaneous and done quite unconsciously.' This does not mean that the same advice is true of older children in a school setting who may well need special language teaching.

The other question about learning a second language that sometimes bothers people is whether speaking two languages holds the child back in some way. Research with school children in Canada, however, suggests almost the opposite. Children who speak two languages do better at intelligence tests; they are more flexible mentally; they are often at a higher stage of mental development. There are, however, two important qualifications to be made. One is that children need to get beyond a certain stage in the second language before these advantages start to show; up to that stage their second language may well handicap them. The other takes up the earlier point that children need to see the second language as an alternative to their mother tongue, not as a substitute for it. If they feel themselves threatened by the new language, they will not benefit by learning it. Other things being equal, it is an advantage for children to speak more than one language, if certain conditions are met.

3   Does it matter how my child speaks?

This question usually comes from people who are worried that their children are picking up a kind of English that they think is socially undesirable: they are not speaking 'proper'. A full answer is given in chapter 5. Briefly, children learn the kind of English that they hear around them; if they hear people saying 'I didn't do nuffing to nobody', they will say 'I didn't do nuffing to nobody'. They're learning the kind of language that goes with a particular group that they meet, with which they want to identify themselves. If a parent does not like this group, the only real solution is to change the kind of people the child encounters or admires and hence the kind of language he hears. If this is not possible, parents can perhaps console themselves with the thought that children are adaptable and when they feel they belong to a different group, their language will change accordingly. The alternative solution of trying to correct the child's speech may on the one hand be seen by the child as a threat to his identity and may on the other hand have little effect in the face of the pressure from everything else the child is hearing. Certain kinds of English do seem part of the entry qualifications for certain professions but the child will still have plenty of time to adapt himself in later life if necessary. Think for instance of the voices of British actors in 1950s films compared with the voices of the same actors in films made in the 1970s; there is a world of difference. The voices have changed to suit the times. Even adults can adapt their kind of speech within certain limits, if they find it necessary, as many British politicians bear witness.

If, however, parents are still determined to make their children sound like the members of some group they admire, there is one more warning to give. This is that they should be quite certain that the aspects of the child's speech that they pick on are really those that people notice. The famous points that people talk about such as dropping 'h's, using 'isn't' rather than 'ain't', having one negative in a sentence rather than several, are fairly small in number. If you are really going to change the way that someone speaks you are going to have to do a lot more than eliminate these. In addition many of the points that people are aware of can be extremely misleading. Take the statement that educated people do not drop their 'h's. Many people are firmly convinced that this is true and are insulted if you tell them that they drop theirs. But try listening to what people actually say rather than taking their word for it and you find that everybody drops some 'h's; it is almost impossible to say 'he had half-starved his horse' and to pronounce each 'h'. What *is* true is that different kinds of accent drop their 'h's differently; if the above sentence is said rapidly almost everybody would leave out the 'h's in 'had' and 'his' but only speakers of certain kinds of English would leave out the 'h's in 'half' and 'horse'. All in all it seems better to let the kind of English the child uses take care of itself. This does not mean of course that one will allow the child to get away with expressions that are a deliberate provocation; the child can try things on with language just as much as with behaviour.

4   What should I do with a child who does not speak in a playgroup?

Playgroup supervisors have often asked me what to do with a child who does not seem to use language at the playgroup. As usual it is hard to give a general answer because children are individuals. There are many reasons why a child does not speak and consequently many ways of getting him to speak. Some children have genuine mental or physical problems with language and in this case the playgroup leader should get professional advice from people qualified to deal with children's speech. Health visitors or health centres will be able to say where this advice is available. There are, however, other causes which are simpler to handle.

The first thing is to make sure that the child is really not speaking. He may not be speaking to one playgroup leader or to some of the children but this does not mean that he is equally taciturn with all the adults or all the children. It is worth observing the child to see whether his apparent lack of speech is in fact real. The second thing to check is whether this lack of speech goes along with a lack of comprehension. If the child joins in and understands what is going on around him and what is said to him, this is rather different from a child who uses language neither for speaking nor for understanding. The third thing to notice is the child's character. Children differ from each other as much as adults in some ways. Some people talk a lot, some hardly open their mouths and this does not necessarily show anything more than a difference in their personalities. For teachers it is often a surprise when the best essay comes from a quiet student who sits at the back of the class and seldom joins in what is happening. Silence does not necessarily show that the child is not participating and benefiting from what is going on.

Apart from personality factors, the other likely cause of the child's not speaking is the difference between the situations that he is used to and the situation of the playgroup. Perhaps he needs time to adjust to being in a room with a lot of other children. Perhaps the kind of English used in the home is different from that in the playgroup and he needs time to acclimatize himself, particularly if English is seldom heard in the home, as is the case with children of non-English speaking parents. Or the kind of relationship he is used to having with adults may be different, or the attitudes to toys and the games he is used to playing. The first step is to try to pinpoint the probable reason for the child's lack of speech in the playgroup situation. The cure depends on the reason but once again the theme from the last chapter should be mentioned: the most important thing is talking to the child as an individual. Bearing this in mind, several approaches are possible. If it is the strangeness of being with other children that is affecting him, this may be helped partly by encouraging his mother to stay and play alongside him for a longer settling-in time than usual, partly by starting him off with activities that only involve himself, such as painting, or a few other children, such as building with bricks, rather than activities where he has to play with a large group of children. Other children, however, may find themselves more at ease in large group activities where they do not have to act or think for themselves. If the basic reason is more the child's personality and shyness, then some thought should be given to activities which overcome this shyness. One stand-by is glove or finger puppets; children sometimes find it easier to talk to a puppet the adult is working than to the adult herself; alternatively the child can work the puppet and make it say things himself. Another mainstay is the various chanting and counting games that the child can take part in. It may also be a good idea to persuade the child's mother to do the same activities at home so that the child finds something similar in both situations. But the most important thing with all of these is not to let the child become too aware of what you are trying to do. If he thinks you are getting at his language, whether by practicing it or correcting it constantly, this may well turn something that is only a temporary problem of adjustment to a new situation into something more serious and more lasting.

5   Are some children deprived of language?

Many people have hotly debated the question whether some
children are so starved of language that they do not learn to use
language normally – that they have 'language deprivation'. The
conclusion one comes to is very much a matter of opinion and
depends largely on how one defines the word 'deprivation.' To
some people it means that the child hears no language at all and it
is certainly true that in that case the child does not learn to speak
normally. To others it is more a question of degree; some children
get more language than others and this gives them an advantage.
The quarrel is really over how much language is needed by the
child and how many children do not get what they need. There is
still no conclusive answer to either of these questions.

The main difficulty is deciding what things are 'deprivation'
and what things are 'difference'. Chapter 5 pointed out that
speaking a different kind of language did not necessarily mean
speaking an inferior kind of language. It is easy for the speaker of
'standard' English to misinterpret other kinds of English or of
behaviour as being deprived. Many of the arguments about
deprivation are also arguments about non-standard speakers
whose language differs significantly from the standard. For
example the fact that a child is slow to volunteer information may
mean that in his usual environment children are not expected to
contribute things of their own to discussions, rather than that he
is deprived. Since non-standard speech often goes along with low
social status, it is also accompanied by other kinds of deprivation
such as poor housing and low income. But language deprivation
does not belong in the same category. A middle-class child who
spends his day with an au-pair girl may be more deprived of
language than a working-class child who spends it with a
childminder; at least the minder usually speaks the same
language! There is no direct reason why economic deprivation
should go with language deprivation.

But of course there may be indirect reasons. For another way
of looking at deprivation is to consider it from the point of view of
the individual child in a particular family rather than the child as

a member of a social group. Earlier chapters have shown how complicated language development is. It may be that some aspects of it depend upon the child having certain relationships with adults at the crucial time. If it is important for the child to play with language by producing nonsense songs and made-up words, he is not likely to thrive in a household where such frivolous activities are frowned upon. So the different types of relationship he is forming, the different routines he has for interacting with people, may affect his language development to a greater or lesser degree. A particular family, because of its circumstances and the personalities that make it up, may put more stress on some aspects of language and less stress on others. If a child is never talked *to*, never treated as an individual, in our culture it is likely that his language will not develop as rapidly. The more strain the adults are under, the more likely his language as well as his other needs will be neglected. So, although it cannot be said he is deprived in the sense that he does not hear *any* language, he is certainly deprived in the sense that he is not given the full range of language that other children have. Certain family circumstances give the child a less rich language environment than others. Undoubtedly factors such as stress and strain in his parents may have this effect and this may be caused among other things by difficulty with money or somewhere to live. So economic deprivation might indirectly lead to deficiencies in what the child hears. But these deficiencies can equally well be caused by other aspects of the child's situation. The remedy was suggested in chapter 7 – give the child as rich a language experience as possible, above all by talking to him as an individual. But of course this only goes some way towards a solution as the underlying cause is not simply the parents' language but the parents' circumstances and personalities. It should perhaps be emphasized, however, that there is still no certain evidence whether children are deprived of particular aspects of language, partly because we do not know what factors in the language the child hears are important to his development.

Further reading

Most of the up-to-date books on the language of young children are rather technical or deal with children of school age. The following books, however, are not only readable but also sensible.

J. G. de Villiers and P. A. de Villiers, *Language Acquisition* (Harvard University Press, 1978). An excellent overview of children's language but expensive.
M. Donaldson, *Children's Minds* (Fontana, 1978). A very interesting paperback about the child's mental development.
L. Berg, *Look at Kids.* (Penguin, 1972). A child-centred deeply-committed book, though not particularly about language.

Books about reading
D. Moyle, *The Teaching of Reading* (Ward Lock, 1968)
D. Mackay, B. Thompson and P. Schaub, *Breakthrough to Literacy: Teacher's Manual* (Longman, 1970)
V. Southgate and G. Roberts, *Reading: Which Approach?* (University of London Press, 1970)

Books with rhymes and songs
The Oxford Book of Nursery Rhymes, assembled by I. Opie and P. Opie (Oxford University Press)
B. Wildsmith, *Mother Goose* (Oxford University Press)
Out of the Pumpkin Shell: Running a Women's Liberation Playgroup (Birmingham Women's Liberation, 65 Prospect Road, Moseley, Birmingham 13)
J. Dakin, *Songs and Rhymes for the Teaching of English* (Longman)
S. Milligan, *Silly Verse for Kids* (Penguin)

Books for under-fives

This is simply a personal list of some of the books that I have found useful with under-fives, for one reason or another.

A. Ahlberg, *The Brick Street Boys* (Collins)

Q. Blake, *Snuff* (Puffin)

M. Bond, *Olga Makes a Wish* (Penguin)

P. Breinburg, *My Brother Sean* (Puffin)

R. Briggs, *Father Christmas* (Puffin)

J. Burmingham, *The Baby*

P. Cameron, *The Cat who Thought he was a Tiger* (Puffin)

E. Carle, *The Mixed-Up Chameleon* (Hamish Hamilton)

F. Dickens, *Albert Herbert Hawkins: The Naughtiest Boy in the World* (Piccolo)

P. Dickinson, *The Iron Lion* (Allen and Unwin)

M. Foreman, *All the King's Horses* (Hamish Hamilton)

S. Gretz, *The Bears who Went to the Seaside* (Puffin)

Grimm Brothers, *Household Tales* (Picador)

J. Kent, *The Blah* (Abelard-Schumann)

R. Kraus, *Whose Mouse are You?* (Puffin)

A. Lindgren, *The Fox and the Tomten* (Armada)

H. Nicoll and J. Pienkowski, *Meg and Mog* (Puffin)

M. Peake, *Captain Slaughterboard Drops Anchor* (Acadamy)

C. Ryan, *Hildelid's Night* (Collins)

M. Sendak, *In the Night Kitchen* (Puffin)

M. Thaler, *How far will a rubber band stretch?* (Collins)

D. and A. Trez, *Circus in the Jungle* (Faber and Faber)

T. Ungerer, *Zeralda's Ogre* (Puffin)

P. Woolcott, *Where did that naughty little hamster go?* (Addison-Wesley)

T. and W. Zacharias, *But where is the green parrot?* (Piccolo)

References

The following lists give the sources that were drawn upon in the various chapters of this book and add one or two books that are also relevant.

Chapter 1. Starting to use language
Bruner, J. S., 'From Communication to Language: A Psychological Perspective,' *Cognition* 3/3, 1974/5.
Eimas, P. D., Siqueland, E. R., Jusczyk and Vigorito, J., 'Speech perception in infants,' *Science* 171, 1971.
Greenfield, P. M. and Smith, J. H., *The Structure of Communication in Early Language Development*, London: Academic Press, 1976.
Halliday, M. A. K., *Learning How to Mean*, London: Edward Arnold, 1975.
Nelson, K., *Structure and Strategy in Learning to Talk*, Monographs of the Society for Research in Child Development No. 149, 1973.
Oller, D. K., Wieman, L. A., Doyle, W. J. and Ross, C., 'Infant babbling and speech,' *Journal of Child Language*, 3, 1976.
Shatz, M., 'On the development of communicative understandings; an early strategy for interpreting and responding to messages,' *Cognitive Psychology* 10, 1978.
Sinclair, H., 'Sensorimotor Action Patterns as a Condition for the Acquisition of Syntax,' in Huxley, R., and Ingram, E., (eds.) *Language Acquisition: Models and Methods*, London: Academic Press, 1971.
Trevarthen, C., 'Conversations with a two-month-old,' *New Scientist* 62, 1974.

Chapter 2. Starting to organise sentences
Bloom, L., *One Word at a Time*, The Hague: Mouton, 1973.

Braine, M. D. S., *Children's First Word Combinations*, Monographs of the Society for Research in Child Development No. 164, 1976.

Brown, R. W., *A First Language: The Early Stages*, London: Allen & Unwin, 1974.

Clark, H. H. and Clark, E. V., *Psychology and Language*, London: Harcourt Brace Jovanovich, 1977.

de Villiers, J. G. and de Villiers, P. A., 'A Cross-sectional Study of Grammatical Morphemes in Child Speech,' *Journal of Psycholinguistic Research* 2, 1973.

Howe, C. J., 'The meanings of two-word utterances in the speech of young children,' *Journal of Child Language* 3, 1976.

Weir, R. H., *Language in the Crib*, The Hague: Mouton, 1962.

Chapter 3. Developing up to five

Bloom, L., *Language Development: Form and Function in Emerging Grammars*, London: MIT, 1970.

Brown, R., 'The development of wh questions in child speech,' *Journal of Verbal Learning and Verbal Behaviour* 7, 1968.

Cook, V. J., 'A note on indirect objects,' *Journal of Child Language* 3, 1976.

Keenan, E. O. and Klein, E., 'Coherency in children's discourse,' *Journal of Psycholinguistic Research* 4, 1975.

Schachter, F. F., Kirshner, K., Klips, B. and Sanders, K., *Everyday Preschool Interpersonal Speech Usage; Methodological, Developmental and Sociolinguistic Studies*, Monographs of the Society for Research in Child Development No. 156, 1974.

Sinclair, H. and Bronckart, J. P., 'SVO a linguistic universal?' *Journal of Experimental Child Psychology* 14, 1972.

Slobin, D. I., 'Grammatical transformations and sentence comprehension in childhood and adulthood,' *Journal of Verbal Learning and Verbal Behaviour* 5, 1966.

Tyack, D. and Ingram, D., 'Children's production and comprehension of questions,' *Journal of Child Language* 4, 1977.

Chapter 4. Meaning, thinking and language

Bryant, P., *Perception and Understanding in Young Children*, Methuen, 1974.

Clark, E. V., 'On the acquisition of the meaning of "before" and "after",' *Journal of Verbal Learning and Verbal Behaviour* 10, 1971.

Cromer, R., 'The development of language and cognition: the cognition hypothesis,' in Foss, B., (ed.) *New Perspectives in Child Development*, Harmondsworth: Penguin, 1974.

Hooton, A. B., and Hooton, C., 'The influence of syntax on visual perception,' *Anthropological Linguistics* 19, 1977.

Luria, A. R. and Yudovitch, *Speech and the Development of Mental Processes in the Child*, Harmondsworth: Penguin, 1971.

Lyons, J., *Introduction to Theoretical Linguistics*, London: CUP, 1968.

Olson, G. M., 'Developmental changes in memory and the acquisition of language,' in Moore, T. E. (ed.), *Cognitive Development and the Acquisition of Language*, London: Academic Press, 1973.

Piaget, J. and Inhelder, B., *The Psychology of the Child*, 1969.

Sinclair-de-Zwart, H., 'Developmental Psycholinguistics,' in Elkind, D., and Flavell, J. H. (eds.) *Studies in Cognitive Development*, 1969.

Sinha, C. and Walkerdine, V., *Functional and perceptual aspects of the acquisition of spatial relational terms*. Mimeo.

Chapter 5. The different kinds of language

Berko-Gleason, J., 'Code-switching in children's language,' in Moore, T. E. (ed.) *Cognitive Development and the Acquisition of Language*, London: Academic Press, 1973.

Bernstein, B., *Classes, Codes and Control Vol. I*, London: Routledge and Kegan Paul, 1971.

Crystal, D. and Davy, D., *Investigating English Style*, London: Longman, 1969.

Edwards, A. D., *Language in Culture and Class*, London: Heinemann, 1976.

Francis, H., *Language in Teaching and Learning*, London: Allen and Unwin, 1977.

Labov, W., 'The logic of nonstandard English,' reprinted in Cashdan, A. and the Language and Learning Course Team at the Open University, *Language in Education*, London: Routledge and Kegan Paul, 1972.

Newport, E. L., 'Motherese: The speech of mothers to young children,' in N. J. Castellan *et al.*, *Cognitive Theory*, Vol. 2 1976.

Sachs, J. and Devin, J., 'Young children's use of age-appropriate styles in social interaction and role-playing,' *Journal of Child Language* 3, 1976.

Snow, C. E. and Ferguson, C. A. (eds.), *Talking to Children*, London: CUP, 1977.

Stubbs, M., *Language, schools, and classrooms*, London: Methuen, 1976.

Trudgill, P., *Accent, Dialect and the School*, London: Edward Arnold, 1975.

Chapter 6. Language development after five

Bousfield, W. A., Esterson, J. and Whitmarsh, G. A., 'A study of developmental changes in conceptual and perceptual associative clustering,' *Journal of Genetic Psychology* 92, 1958.

Bruner, J., 'Language as an instrument of thought,' in Davies, A. (ed.) *Problems of Language and Learning*, London: Heineman, 1975.

Conrad, R., 'The chronology of the development of covert speech in children,' *Developmental Psychology* 5, 1971.

Cook, V. J., 'Strategies in the comprehension of relative clauses,' *Language and Speech* 18, 1975.

Cromer, R. F., 'Children are nice to understand: surface structure clues to the recovery of a deep structure,' *British Journal of Psychology* 61, 1970.

Ervin, S., 'Changes with age in the verbal determinants of word association,' *American Journal of Psychology* 74, 1961.

Hagen, J. W., 'Some thoughts on how children learn to remember,' *Human Development* 14, 1971.

Sinclair, J. and Coulthard, M., *Towards an analysis of discourse: the English used by teachers and pupils*. Oxford: OUP, 1974.

Stolz, M. and Tiffany, J., 'The production of "childlike" word associations by adults to unfamiliar adjectives,' *Journal of Verbal Learning and Verbal Behaviour* 11, 1972.

Chapter 7. Helping the under-fives

Cooper, J., Moodley, M. and Reynell, J., *Helping Language*

Development, London: Edward Arnold, 1978.

Downes, G., *Language Development and the Disadvantaged Child*, Edinburgh: Holmes McDougall, 1978.

Gahagan, D. M. and Gahagan, G. A., *Talk Reform*, London: Routledge and Kegan Paul, 1970.

Tizard, B., Cooperman, O., Joseph, A. and Tizard, J., 'Environmental effects on language development; a study of young children in long-stay residential nurseries,' *Child Development* 43, 1972.

Whitehurst, G. J., Novak, G. and Zorn, G. A., 'Delayed speech studied in the home', *Developmental Psychology* 7, 1972.

Chapter 8. Questions and answers

Ben-Zeev, S., 'Mechanisms by which childhood bilingualism affects understanding of language and cognitive structures,' in Hornby, P. A., (ed.) *Bilingualism*, London: Academic Press, 1977.

Cook, V. J., Long, J. and McDonough, S., 'The relationship between first and second language learning,' *Proceedings of the First Assembly of the National Congress on Languages in Education*, Centre for Information on Language Teaching, to appear.

Dartigue, E., 'Bilingualism in the nursery school', *French Review* 39, 1966.

Lambert, W. E., 'Cultural and language factors in learning and education,' in F. Aboud and R. Meade, (eds.) *The Fifth Western Symposium on Learning*, 1974.

Tough, J., *Listening to Children Talking*, London: Ward Lock, 1976.

Index